COMING FULL CIRCLE THROUGH CHANGES, CHALLENGES AND TRANSITIONS

a four quadrant process for
living the examined life

IONE JENSON

BALBOA.
PRESS
A DIVISION OF HAY HOUSE

Balboa Press books may be ordered through booksellers or by contacting:

Balboa Press
A Division of Hay House
1663 Liberty Drive
Bloomington, IN 47403
www.balboapress.com
1 (877) 407-4847

Because of the dynamic nature of the Internet, any web addresses or links contained in this book may have changed since publication and may no longer be valid. The views expressed in this work are solely those of the author and do not necessarily reflect the views of the publisher, and the publisher hereby disclaims any responsibility for them.

The author of this book does not dispense medical advice or prescribe the use of any technique as a form of treatment for physical, emotional, or medical problems without the advice of a physician, either directly or indirectly. The intent of the author is only to offer information of a general nature to help you in your quest for emotional and spiritual well-being. In the event you use any of the information in this book for yourself, which is your constitutional right, the author and the publisher assume no responsibility for your actions.

Any people depicted in stock imagery provided by Thinkstock are models, and such images are being used for illustrative purposes only.
Certain stock imagery © Thinkstock.

Print information available on the last page.

ISBN: 978-1-5043-2857-9 (sc)
ISBN: 978-1-5043-2859-3 (hc)
ISBN: 978-1-5043-2858-6 (e)

Library of Congress Control Number: 2015903016

Balboa Press rev. date: 03/16/2015

To my husband Asa for his
unfaltering support,
and
For my sons, Charles and Allan,
grandchildren Karl, Olivia and Emma, and
to my dear friend Masil Hulse and all those
souls brave enough to live the examined life.

CONTENTS

PREFACE

The Spiritual Journey requires commitment if
We're serious about wanting to grow our soul.
-Ione Jenson

My own spiritual quest has been going on for as long as I can remember. Even as a very small child growing up in the Midwest, I remember lying on a blanket in our backyard on hot sultry summer evenings when it was too warm to go into the house before midnight. There was no air conditioning back then, so for the three summer months I spent most of my nights staring at the stars and moon in the black sky and wondering about all the secrets God had hidden up there.

As a young adult I began my search to know God and to understand the mystery of the cosmos. I tried searching first in the church where answers were elusive and often were given to me in pious platitudes. Then I tried psychology where I began finding some answers but they were mostly devoid of any spiritual dimension. Later I found the works of Carl Jung who introduced the spiritual element into psychology, but I found that at a much later time and after I had found a group in Eugene, Oregon who called themselves "Discovery." It was made up of people from many denominations in the Christian traditions and all were seeking a deeper understanding of "Life." It was my salvation in many ways, but I knew that somehow the physical life, the psychological life and the spiritual life were interrelated.

In setting out to find how I could put this together in my personal journey, I discovered many bits and pieces that I could use and weave together to make a more complete and workable way of living. This was during the 1960's and 1970's before the Holistic approach was as widely visible as it would later become. It was a time of searching for many people and especially true of the "counter culture" generation. I tried to learn as many techniques and understand as many philosophies as I could. It was a rich period in my life when every day held new discoveries and wonders. I found real "gems" in many diverse places and learned from the workshops and classes that were beginning to abound by the late 1970's and early 1980's. All of these were separate experiences and stood alone. There were Value Clarification classes, Behavior Modification techniques, Reality Therapy, Dream Workshops, Journaling Seminars, Meditation Retreats, and a host of other choices such as: EST, Gestalt Therapy, Sensitivity Sessions, Rebirthing methods, Assertive Training, and the power of Visualization to name a few. All added immensely to my search, and I found that by blending many of them together and using them in tandem at times, my life became more conscious and purposeful, and I was becoming less and less a "victim of fate." In fact, I came eventually to understand that I was the creator of my life circumstances and the scripture: As a man thinks, so is he" became clear in a way I'd never understood before. As the wife of a minister, I began to teach classes at the church, and this opened the doors to allow others to understand their lives in a new way.

In 1975, Masil, a woman in the church where my husband was pastor, had come to me with some issues she needed help solving. In the process of talking with her, she also revealed a physical condition that she had lived with for 16 years. As we began working with some visual imagery techniques, we discovered a powerful link between her emotional and physical health. After spending a few sessions working to integrate them, I was led to ask her if she would like to be healed of her physical problem. A nurse by profession, she held the belief that her condition was incurable. She had been diagnosed after multiple doctors, tests and biopsies and had endured the effects of the disease for sixteen years.

We decided to fast and go up into the nearby forest to visualize and affirm that her body was perfect. As our prayer and meditation continued, we begin to both see and feel her body move and respond to the energy flow as it realigned itself. That healing occurred in 1976, and from that day forward she has never again experienced a single symptom of her disease. She is now in her nineties.

Intrigued, she began a deeper spiritual journey and, ultimately, started working with me as I worked with others and as I taught classes. Masil also began to attend the week long seminars that I was participating in and learned more of the alternative approaches to healing as we both expanded our understandings and learned many new ideas and techniques as well.

It must be noted here that our culture was entering into a new cycle of understanding and into a new level of consciousness in the late 1960's and 1970's. Changes were taking place rapidly and each day seemed to bring new concepts that shattered old belief systems. Nothing was coming under greater revision than notions about Health Care. For a large segment of the population the terms Doctor and God had been synonymous. Fortunately people began to see doctors in a far more realistic light and recognize both their humanness and their fallibility as well as their knowledge and expertise.

A new breed of physician began arising in our midst. They were limited in number, but they were open, receptive and practicing a more integrative approach to health care. At the same time, practitioners began to appear who were outside of what was traditionally practiced in Health Care circles, and as with any movement, some were more legitimate than others. My personal preference was to work with the medical professional where needed. We had both doctors and therapists who referred their patients/clients to us for additional help through the newer techniques that were emerging such as visualization, inner child work, dream work, gestalt dialogue techniques, prayer and other modalities that were proving effective in ways that medicine was not addressing.

In one case a young woman, aged 29, was severely injured in a skiing accident and had spent many weeks in a hospital. Having been released from the hospital a few years earlier, she was trying to learn how to live with and manage her constant pain.

She originally came for help with other matters, but as we worked over a period of time with the emotional issues and current problems, I finally asked if I might pray for her back. I acknowledged that her belief system did not include that type of procedure, but the two friends who were with us that evening needed practice. She consented, mostly out of politeness, and we did a simple procedure called "laying-on-of-hands" in religious circles, or "energy transfer" as it was referred to in other traditions. Susan's back begin to respond immediately as we visualized the perfect back while laying our hands on her spinal column. It began to undulate and looked like painless spasms. This physical movement continued for about twenty minutes and then ceased. She was both awed and puzzled.

The following week-end she took a chain saw and cut wood all day Saturday and spent Sunday skiing. She was totally free of pain. That was about 1979. As a result of her own healing, she went to California and spent two years studying in the field of Holistic Health. She eventually became a licensed naturopath and has her own clinic in Montana. Susan's whole story is told in our book: *Emerging Women* (Hay House)

One thing we learned and that has never changed, is that an invisible power and unseen forces work toward our health and wholeness if the right connection is made. I refer to this power as God, and while others may name it differently, we are all talking about the same creative force from which all things arise. I have seen and felt this healing, redemptive force manifest, and its power is beyond comprehension.

The concept of Integrative Medicine embraces the belief that man is composed of body, mind, soul and spirit. It holds that these elements must balance and be in unity for optimum health to occur. Life is meant to find that balance. By 1980 Masil and I both felt called to create a safe place where people could come and deepen their own journeys; thus we began our search for the perfect place to manifest our vision. During the summer of 1980 we meditated and received a general vicinity to explore. We ended up finding the perfect spot in Hayden Lake, Idaho.

Hayden Lake is approximately six miles from Coeur d'Alene and our land was another seven miles further north.

We found five acres of forested land, and in 1981 we built a facility which included a large solarium giving one the feeling of being among the trees even while in the building. A few years later, we also added a wing with an indoor heated swimming pool. In the fall of 1982, Julie Keene, a Unity minister, joined us and was with us until 1988; she returned again from 1991 to 1998. During those later years, Julie and I wrote two books that were published by Hay House. (*Women Alone: Creating a Joyous and Fulfilling Life, and Emerging Women: the Widening Stream.*) The Holo Center ministry continued for twenty-three years and people flew in from all over the United States and even from Australia and Switzerland when our books became available overseas. Our goal at the Holo Center was to teach people techniques they could employ when they returned home and that would empower them to help themselves.

In 2003, Masil and I sold the Holo Center to retire (more or less) from the never ending work of such an endeavor. People would stay with us for one to three weeks as we worked intensively with them, so it was a 24/7 process. It provided a wonderful Haven for those who needed it, but became more physical work than either Masil or I wanted to give. It was time to move on to the next phase of our journeys. However, during those twenty-three years, we honed our knowledge, understanding, techniques and skills in helping people come into a greater state of wholeness.

During those years at the Holo Center, we found that even though people responded to different techniques to arrive at becoming more integrated, there are four basic and general components that exist in the process. That is what this book attempts to convey. My prayer is always "teach me to think as God thinks, to love as God loves and show me how I can best serve God and Humanity." This book is my attempt to do all three.

INTRODUCTION

People often find it easier to become victims,
Than it is to take responsibility.
-Ione Jenson

Over the last decades many people have become more cognizant of monitoring their emotional health and of recognizing the factors that have contributed to their adult patterns of behavior. This increased knowledge and self-awareness has been healthy and good. However, as is often the case when the pendulum has been leaning too far in one direction, it tends to swing to its opposite extreme. So as an awareness of the impact made by events of the past and the realization of the wounded inner child who needs healing has replaced the earlier unhealthy repressive trends, we have had a tendency to go to the opposite extreme by removing all personal responsibility. While it is important to understand our personal past and work toward integrating its dysfunctional aspects, we need not buy into the unhealthy habit of consistently placing all the blame on the wounds of childhood and allowing those circumstances to give us an excuse for being immobilized or for displaying irresponsible behaviors in the present.

Carolyn Myss (*Why Some People Don't Heal and How They Can* - Harmony Books 1997) calls this kind of behavior *woundology* and believes too many people have become addicted to their personal wounds. The truth is, that everyone has wounds or challenges to overcome; changes, challenges and transitions are a part of this journey called "life," and to live a life of personal integrity, at some point, we must garner courage and move on. We are never absolved or exempt from taking responsibility for our lives, and while we often cannot control some of the events that occur in our outer world, we can take personal responsibility for what we do with them.

While we may say that we would love to be free of anxieties and live an uncomplicated serene life, the truth is that many of us are addicted to emotional crisis because life seems boring and humdrum if things stay on an even keel. If we are not in a swirl of complications in our lives, what is there to talk about or to get others involved with us? Even though it may be unconscious, we will allow our lives to remain uncomplicated for only so long, and then if nothing is happening, we will stir" something up to make our lives more exciting. This type of behavior is toxic.

Most leaders in the self-help movement may not have intended for the addiction to woundology to happen, but as it has evolved, that seems too often to be what occurs. Even some well-meaning therapists and counselors have perpetuated this misguided line of thinking. For one thing, it keeps clients returning which is a therapist's livelihood, and I suppose there is always the possibility that a certain number of unscrupulous counselors might keep the "drama" going endlessly for that reason, but even beyond that, there most often lies a lack of true understanding. Getting caught up or enmeshed in the dramas and crisis can be a real "high" for both client and therapist.

The creation of Women's Centers and Crisis Lines has been a huge blessing, and these centers render a great service. However, my observations have occasionally brought to my awareness that a few of the advocates, usually in the form of volunteers, who are working in various Women's Centers seem to gain a level of questionable excitement from the vicarious experience of crisis in their clients' lives. Sometimes people who are older and retired, or who are housewives looking for meaningful work to do, sign up as volunteers to help women who have experienced rape or domestic violence. More than once when I have been with some of these women in social situations, it has been interesting to note that while they sigh and act utterly exhausted by their volunteer activities, they suddenly take on an aura of exuberance and their faces light up when they begin to explain the horrible situations of the women they are helping. An air of excitement seems to flow through the message even though they are deploring the situation. I honestly believe the conditions some women live under are unbelievably bad, but as certain volunteers are attempting to explain just how bad the conditions are, one can, none-the-less, notice that the volunteer "helpers" are obviously experiencing a level of vicarious excitement. The facial expressions and the tones and inflections of the voice very obviously belie the message they are conveying.

Changes, challenges and transitions can all be motivating factors if we become consciously aware of the opportunities and gifts they offer and move to constructively use them both to heal and to motivate us to reach and stretch beyond our current limited perceptions. Living a serene life does not in any way imply that we must withdraw from life and live as an ascetic or recluse in some distant spiritual setting. However, it does mean that while we can fully embrace all the complexities and the full range of human emotions, we can, none-the-less, grow in confidence and faith and in the ways that we allow the events of our lives to impact us. Honoring inner processes, yet taking full responsibility for changing and recreating one's life is the only way in which healing and progress will ever take place.

In traveling around the country, I once talked with a woman who seemed to epitomize what I call the "victim mentality." She had chosen to have a child alone. It was a conscious decision. As she sat talking, she said that she wanted to buy her own house, she wanted a new car, wanted to maintain an office for a small business, and wanted to continue her college education toward a B.A. degree in Social Work. All admirable goals. However, she climaxed all this by saying she didn't want to work or be involved too many hours a week (maybe 20) because she wanted to spend lots of time with her son while he was small. She was in tears and frustrated because she couldn't have it all; she was tired of the struggle and thought she might be blocking her prosperity consciousness.

Undoubtedly she had some inner programming that did block her prosperity in certain ways, most of us do. But there were other things to be considered as well. It seems to me that she had an unrealistic picture going here. She looked around and saw friends who had more than she did. Some of them were married and had combined incomes to work with; some of them were single, but they were already professionals with college degrees who had worked long hard hours to attain their place in life. Others had chosen to wait until they had partners before parenting or had chosen not to be a sole parent. Still others had worked at steady jobs that provided them with a regular income and certain benefits while investing in their future. And certainly they had all worked more than 20 hours a week. This woman had apparently done none of this.

She described herself as a "free spirit." She said she had never held a salaried job, but had dabbled in a number of different activities, traveled extensively attending personal and spiritual growth seminars while living life her way." I applaud her decision to forego the traditional structured lifestyle, if that's what she wanted to do, and appreciated her desire to fully experience a multitude of adventures. It's a wonderful way to get a rich and varied education, and I made a similar choice back in 1976 when I left full-time employment in the field of education in order to free-lance. Her story is not unusal and many have opted for those same choices.

However, there are choices to make when we determine to walk a path similar to hers. We need to clarify our values and rank them in order of importance. Then each choice we make must support those values. It follows that while we can have anything we really want, we probably are not going to be able to have everything we want all at once. As we make certain choices, it's entirely possible that other choices may have to be set aside for a time. Life is full of options, but some options are mutually exclusive of other options. For example, if we decide that we want to earn a lot of money, we will probably have to work for it. A full time job is most likely going to prevent us from taking extended vacations and from spending unlimited time just loafing. On the other hand, if we choose to travel and relax for a good share of the time and are not financially independent or wealthy, we may have to find ways of traveling on a shoestring and cutting other expenses to a minimum in order to afford the luxury of a relaxed easy-going lifestyle. That does not seem difficult to comprehend.

All people, no matter what their income, do have to make choices at some level. There are many non-economic related choices that everyone must consider also; we are always making pivotal decisions. The real tragedy occurs when we are unwilling to accept responsibility for our choices and unwilling to think through both the short and long term consequences of what we do.

Life is never just plain luck, rather it's a combination of effort and the willingness to create and seize opportunities through skillful decision making. While many people are taking the responsibility for creating a joyous and fulfilling life, others are still hanging around waiting for it to "happen" to them or making excuses why it can't or doesn't occur. Some people are unaware that they can create their own healing and build a meaningful existence for themselves, while still others have misread or misinterpreted certain new age concepts and mistakenly think that desiring and affirming what they want requires no further action. While there are certain aspects of truth to that concept, and both desires and affirmations are powerful aids in creating our life, it does not let us off the hook for taking our share of responsibility in the process.

The following story best illustrates our "response-ability" for making things happen in our lives. It seems there was a huge flood, and as the water was rising around his house, the owner prayed that God would rescue him. Soon a canoe came by and offered to take him to dry land. He refused and continued to pray that God would save him as the water was rising higher and higher around his house. A motorboat came by and wanted to take the man to dry land, but again he refused and continued to pray asking God to rescue him. Finally, the water was so high that the man was forced to take refuge on his roof. As the water continued to rise to the roof top, a helicopter came and wanted to lift the man to safety. He refused and continued in his prayers asking that God save him. Eventually, the water rose so high that it engulfed the poor fellow and he went under and drowned. When he arrived at heaven's gates he was visibly upset and demanded an explanation as to why God had let him down when he had been faithful in his prayers and in his belief that God would save him. God looked at him and quietly answered: "I did answer your prayers, and I sent a canoe, a motorboat, and a helicopter. You refused to take the step into any of them that would have saved your life."

How often we are like that man. We pray for what we want and need, we expect God to answer and give us what we've asked for, but we aren't willing to cooperate with Divine Forces in order to manifest the answers to the desires of our heart. It's as though we have asked to be the author of a best-selling book but were never willing to put any words on paper.

Young women like this probably can have all of their desires, eventually, if they takes time to define their values and goals, explore options and make some decisions about immediate priorities. They can then begin to work toward the most important objectives while accepting the fact that in order to have what is most important to them in the present moment, they need to be willing to temporarily postpone other desires. One-by-one, it is possible to accomplish each goal in its own time and avoid both stressing out and sinking into the feeling of defeat over the inability to manifest the whole list immediately.

It is often evident that people are not seeking possible solutions but have fallen into a victim mentality. Many would prefer to have sympathy or a spiritual miracle that would eliminate the arduous task of soul development that comes with being responsible for helping to bring about one's own good.

The emotional, physical, mental, and spiritual aspects of life cannot be separated; they are a part of an integral whole. Each challenge in our life holds components of these four area's and must all be confronted in order to achieve wholeness. Each area contains its own seed for our growth potential, and together they are the garden of the soul.

Encouraging people to take responsibility and action by devising a plan, however small, that moves them toward their goals, is the most loving advice we can give.

There are always options available in every situation. Even though some of those choices may not be acceptable to us, they force us to continually define and refine our values and priorities. Victor Frankel, the internationally known Viennese psychiatrist, found in the Nazi concentration camps that his captors could imprison his body, but not his mind or attitudes. In choosing to control those two inner aspects of his life, he was able to retain his strength and personhood.

Far too many people are searching for a God that is a benevolent parent and who will give them what they want and ask nothing in return. For them to grasp the concept that God does give us the desires of our hearts, but that God is an energy moving us ever forward in our soul's growth and it is our job to learn the spiritual principles that govern all life, seems too difficult a course to embrace. In many respects our culture seems to have encouraged a victim mentality, and people have, in becoming aware of their "rights," all too often been willing to surrender their responsibility for taking charge of their own lives.

I was made aware of this victim mentality many years ago while visiting a friend in California soon after heavy rains had created a flash flood that ran into her home and that of ten neighbors. All but one of the families had dug in and began the cleanup work. They pulled up carpets, washed down walls, cupboards and closets. In short, they began to immediately clean up, repair and attempt to put their lives back into some semblance of order in so far as possible. No one had flood insurance. A small amount of federal aid did arrive ($5,000 from FEMA) but it didn't come close to covering the damage. However, most of these folks did the best they could and were managing to overcome the disaster.

However, one family made no attempt to clean up any of the muddy waters. They, instead, spent the next few weeks running from agency to agency to complain, to try to get someone to come and clean up the mess for them (after all it was not *their* fault!) and to restore their home to its previous condition. While they complained, made numerous phone calls and appeared at various agencies, the water damage further deteriorated their house. While ten families had all been able to minimize the flood water's damage, this family allowed standing water to warp the structure and the ensuing mold to further demolish their premises. They did not qualify nor get the additional services they requested, and by not cleaning up as their neighbors had done, they compounded their problems. They relinquished their responsibility to do what they could, and then spent their time in a badly damaged house and going from neighbor to neighbor for sympathy and support in denouncing the "government" for not rescuing them from the challenges they faced.

Back then my friend summed the situation up by saying: "You know, they are in their forties and the rest of us are all close to 60. I think the difference is simply that we were raised before government entitlements and we don't expect someone to take care of us. We were always taught that you get in and do what you can to help yourself, and then, if someone helps you, it's a gift, not their obligation to "fix it" for you." I think my friend's observations are quite accurate. We do occasionally need help, and as fellow humans we do need to help one another, but that does not relieve us of the responsibility of helping ourselves. Going back to the early days of our country's history, can you imagine the neighbors coming in for a barn raising or the building of a log cabin while the landowner sat under a tree because he did not feel it was his responsibility to provide shelter for his family or livestock? It sounds absurd doesn't it? But it is exactly what my friend's neighbor was attempting to do.

It seems like one of the big lessons during this period of history is to regain our sense of self-reliance, to restore the dignity of self-respect that comes from being able to care for ourselves and to find creative ways to overcome life's trials and obstacles. And while we do not want to sacrifice a caring and helping attitude toward those in less fortunate circumstances during the process, it is certainly time to restore a healthy perspective and balance. Perhaps people would be better served if we were teaching them how to take responsibility for themselves. In doing so, we would be helping them to create a shift in perception that would, ultimately, teach them how to better use their energy and to create lives of integrity.

In some of the discussions centering around Welfare Reform, it has been suggested that recipients be required to take money management classes, nutrition training, family planning, stress management, parenting courses, and job skill training among others. In transforming the welfare system, it seems to me the over-all goal has to provide short term help while encouraging long term economic independence. Of course, there are the inevitable catastrophes that occur when we try to fashion one set of rules and apply them to everyone, so we do need some flexibility when applying them across the board. We do need, of course, to also look at the larger problem and level the playing field so that individuals can succeed. However, an individual's self-worth is directly connected to their ability to control and decide the course of their life.

Learning to take responsibility for personal decisions and for creating a rich and fulfilling life needs to begin early. When I taught young children and supervised teachers in early childhood education programs, I always encouraged both teachers and aides to empower children to be independent. It was our "motto," never help children do *anything* that they could be doing for themselves. While this approach never denied a child the help they really needed, it did call for the adults to pause and evaluate how necessary help was and to encourage the child to do all or whatever part of the task they were capable of doing for themselves. It was tremendous to see the amount of independence and the capabilities each child displayed before the end of the school year. Perhaps, if we as a culture could use the same measuring stick when helping adults, (because most dependent behavior in adult life is a return to the child-like ways of helplessness) we could empower people to be courageous and autonomous. For anyone reading these pages who would like to know just how to begin teaching sound decision making skills to children, I urge you to read: *Parenting with Love and Logic* by Foster Cline and Jim Fey.

Often people we talk to, read about, or see on TV carry much the same attitude. I once watched an interview with a middle aged man. He apparently had been employed at a good job with a six figure income and had lost it during the company's down-sizing a few months earlier. He was despondent and in tears. He had sent out numerous resumes and had job interviews, but had been unable to find a new position in his field. He had a very large home, three children in college, several expensive late-model cars in the driveway and no job or money to maintain any of it. He was in a heavy personal depression. The interview was designed to give America a view of the economic depression, and it accomplished that goal.

However, it also gave Americans an opportunity to see something else. While empathizing with the man's position, I did not only see him as the economic victim that was being portrayed on my screen that evening, but even more as a victim of his own lack of creative thinking. He victimized himself by his inability to seize the challenge and by his failure to consider there might be a bigger picture.

It did not seem apparent during the course of the interview that this man was even aware of possible alternatives to despondency. He did not seem to grasp that college students all over America go to college without owning expensive late model cars and his children could do likewise. My son finished college just a year before that interview took place, and he never had a car the entire four years but used public transportation instead. It never seemed to occur to this man that his children might take some responsibility for earning their own college tuition and the experience might even be an important part of their educational process. Many of us have children who have had to take student loans and work part time jobs in order to get their degrees. His children might be richer in the long run for having this experience as well. Also, it didn't seem this gentleman had even considered that a smaller house might be adequate and would cut his payments to a manageable size. Mansions are fun to live in but certainly not essential to happiness. He also had not considered other types of work at less salary until the right thing came along. He didn't seem to have a glimmer that perhaps this challenge was a call to psycho-spiritual growth, or that it might be an opportunity to try some creative endeavor he loved and might never have had the courage to do if it had meant giving up the job and prestige to which he had become accustomed. Wonderful things might have lurked in this situation if only the man could have released the victim mentality long enough to look for possible opportunities. How we view challenges is infinitely more important than the challenge.

This man's story reminded me of an interview I read many years ago in the magazine *Psychology Today*. It told of an older man who loved to garden, but as he aged and his physical capabilities faltered, he downsized his garden. Eventually he went from working a huge garden to planting flowers in a window box. Nothing, not even deteriorating health, could stop him from pursuing his passion. Loss had forced him to re-group, but he still retained the power to choose how he would respond.

In 1985 my then 23 year old son, Allan, had just been discharged from the Navy and had found in his exit physical that he tested HIV Positive. Allan returned home and begin to process the information. During a two year period we talked long and frequently. At the end of two years, he called me and told me he had made a decision to live his life, not his death. (At that point it was still a certain "death sentence.") He enrolled at the University of Portland and four years later graduated with a degree in Computer Science. During college, since his finances were tight, he took a job on weekends taking care of city computers and attending classes during the week. He also took student loans. He lived his life fully for the 14 years after diagnosis and almost to the very end. At the end of his 37 years of life, I am quite certain there had been major soul progress.

If we are ever to attain peace, what must take place? We must stop acting the role of victims and begin to take responsibility for evolving our lives consciously. This book is a four part plan for doing just that.

We must surrender our victim mentality and use our inherent creative powers to fashion our lives. This is our soul's journey. Growing our soul is not an end, but a lifelong process. It can be a joyous journey. Stuart Wilde has written a book with the title: "*Life Wasn't Meant to Be a Struggle.*" We are so much more than we think we are. We are rich in latent capacities and we have far more control of our destiny than we actually think we possess.

It is easy to feel victimized, helpless or immobilized. And, unfortunately, there are plenty of people who embrace and perpetuate these myths. Listening and allowing another person to discharge emotions is important, no doubt about it, and reflective therapy which allows people to make discoveries about themselves is also healthy and vital. However, as powerful as those tools are, they can be time consuming and limiting when used solely by themselves. In order for lives to heal and change in positive and lasting directions, several processes need to take place, simultaneously, as we face the lessons and challenges that life presents. It is to that end this book is being written. It is my desire to help ordinary individuals find a road map that leads them to effective and long term change.

Summary

There are different ways that change can be dealt with. Some folks will ignore it and pretend it never occurred, while others will grit their teeth and either rebel or "grin and bear" it. However, some will accept that change in life is inevitable and calls forth our own inner strength, faith and creativity. Seen from a larger perspective, change can be fundamentally good. It offers a chance to be introspective, to learn from the lessons it brings, whether those lessons feel good or not, and to learn that change is an inevitable evolutionary process. If we can change our focus and look at its positive potential, we can see that learning to find both courage and strength in the changes, challenges and transitions of life can bring the wonderful rewards of what may eventually emerge out of those very events. I once had a minister who always said: "We never give up good except for greater good," and I certainly have experienced the truth of that statement over and over again.

It is wise to remember that so many of the great people that we read about throughout history have had to overcome much adversity before attaining their achievements.

CHAPTER ONE

Introduction to the Four Quadrant Process

We create our lives, drawing to us both people and events,
By our words, thoughts and actions.
-Ione Jenson

In 1951, Maslow reported that the healthiest adults in his study were independent, detached, and self-governing. They governed their lives by looking deep inside themselves for what was right, and this was not always or necessarily in alignment with what was culturally popular or socially acceptable. Maslow defined them as autonomous (empowered/ self-actualizing) and found that they had discovered the seeming opposites such as work/play, duty/pleasure, self-interest/altruism, individualism/selflessness to all be the same. Maslow felt that truly healthy people made choices that were good for everyone, not just solely beneficial to themselves. They were able to find win/win solutions to the problems and challenges in life and were able to apply the principles of synergy effectively. They had attained maturity.

Webster's Dictionary defines maturity in the following way. Mature: 1) based on slow, careful considerations; 2) having completed natural growth and development; 3) ripe

We need to ask ourselves: "Am I a mature person? Am I willing to take responsibility for my life, for the choices I make, and am I willing to be responsible for the outcome of those decisions? Am I willing to stop blaming others or life itself for all the things that I don't like or that don't work in my life? Am I willing to look at the people in my life and see how they mirror for me both my own strengths and weaknesses? When I see a weakness reflected, am I willing to honestly stop projecting my self-hatred out onto others and begin learning how to embrace the unlovable within myself? Am I willing to look at not only my self-interest in any given situation, but also look at what is good for the whole, the family, the office staff, my community, my country or humanity at large? Am I willing to give people the benefit of the doubt and listen carefully in order to try to understand their reasons before pressing my arguments on them? Am I willing to remain non-judgmental when another's lifestyle or opinion differs from mine? Am I willing to honor diversity both in other people and in myself? Am I willing to be as honest as possible with myself and in my dealings with other people? Am I willing never to "use" another as a means to personal gain, in any manner, however large or small? Am I willing to confront my fears and insecurities in order to surrender the need for power and control over the lives of others? Am I willing to embrace my truth and base my actions on what I deeply hold to be honest and true regardless of popular opinion?"

Over the past few decades I've discovered the people I've observed, interviewed, or counseled and who live the healthiest, happiest and most productive lives, tend to have four basic things in common. They all know what they value and have strong personal boundaries around those values. They are willing to look at what does and doesn't work in their lives and face the reality of what they need to modify in order to live in integrity and in accordance with their personal value system. They respect their inner processes and understand that many outside factors and cultural influences have molded and shaped them, and they are willing to work toward integration when aspects of themselves are in conflict. They all have a firm belief in something greater than the limits of their own conscious finite minds. They call it by many names: God, Divine Mind, Cosmic Intelligence, Super Conscious, Organic Process, Energy, Wisdom, Synchronicity, or a myriad of other labels, but they all subscribe to the concept that a higher power source turns the universe in some mysterious way and with some semblance of order.

As I have worked through my own processes and have aided countless others in working through theirs, it has become apparent that to use these four processes in tandem is to find a healthy and workable way of life. The order in which these steps are applied will vary from situation to situation, but sooner or later, moving through each step creates a more productive and complete course of action. Two of the processes are essentially left brained and two are right brained although some overlapping may be involved. Finding that delicate but powerful balance between the logic/reasoning and intuitive/feeling components of our brains, the yin and the yang energies, is to find the centered peaceful existence we all crave, and yet, at the same time it allows us to live involved, powerful and effective lives. This is not to say challenges, personal growth, and learning opportunities will not occur, but it is to say that with a predetermined way of confronting issues, we can use them to enhance our personal awareness and for the advancement of our soul growth. In doing so, each experience can lead us deeper into self-knowledge and direct us to ways of enhancing the state of our health and increasing our productivity.

I have made a diagram of the four-quadrant process in this manner:

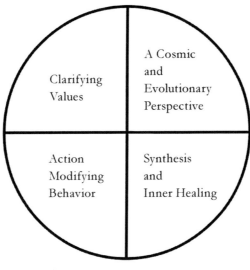

Four Quadrant Process

In the upper left quadrant of the circle we need to sort out our basic *VALUES* and goals. It is essential to be clear with ourselves as to what values we embrace as our own and which ones, perhaps, have been handed to us by our childhood religion, our culture and/or our families. Some of these early values or goals may or may not serve our best interests at this point in our lives, and if we can be clear about what is really important to us, we can live a more integrated life and one of utmost integrity. Unless we know what we value and practice making choices that support those values, it's difficult to respond to life and to crisis in a healthy way.

In the bottom left corner of the circle, we see the process of *ACTION*. Many of our challenges need confronted with realistic evaluation. They often call us to modify our behavior or to take assertive steps in order to create solutions to the dilemmas they pose. While doing nothing about a situation is occasionally the action that needs to be taken, more often, we can release the numerous mind games that roll over and over in our heads if we will just take some constructive steps toward finding a reasonable solution. Often these steps may be very small, but even a small step can make a world of difference in regaining our personal power in adverse circumstances.

The bottom right hand corner is the quadrant of *SYNTHESIS and INNER HEALING*. This quadrant offers many different techniques and possibilities for synthesizing the earlier events in our lives that still color and influence our adult years. There are many ways to gain skill in implementing these techniques for integration. Of course, good therapists are always available, but beyond that, there are workshops, classes and wonderful books dealing with and providing instruction in every one of these techniques. Having entered into this quadrant during the early 1960's when little was available and certainly nothing was being taught on college campus' along these lines, I found a few books and works on Assagioli and psycho-synthesis, did some Gestalt therapy as taught by Fritz Perls, found some books on dream work, universal symbolism and directed daydreams. I also took a few of the early sensitivity sessions. From these I gleaned ideas and often extrapolated those ideas and began my journey into self-understanding and integration. However, if you have any doubts at all about your ability to do this safely, or if you have major emotional or mental challenges, by all means seek the help of someone qualified to lead you through this quadrant.

The fourth and final quadrant located in the upper right hand corner is termed *THE COSMIC OVERVIEW and EVOLUTIONARY PERSPECTIVE*. It is the process which gives me the confidence to begin work on the other three. It is the same process which helps me, when I have come to the end of a challenge, understand the larger meaning behind the lessons I've learned. And it also gives me a perspective beyond the obvious, although sometimes this comes years later. From this quadrant comes my daily spiritual practices and my strength. It does not dictate a universal belief system because my understanding changes and grows as I do. Neither my system of belief nor my daily spiritual practices are exactly like anyone else's, nor should they be. Each of us has our own path and must find a system or journey that speaks deeply to our inner depths. However, this quadrant implies faith in something larger than our finite minds and calls on that power to help guide and expand both our lives and our options.

These four processes can be used every day of our lives. By making them routine, we have an automatic way of responding to the unexpected challenges, both large and small. However, again I would like to make it clear that there is a need for support groups and good therapists of all kinds. One should not hesitate to seek out professional help and expertise when one is going through major crisis or mental disorders. There are times in everyone's life when they would probably profit by talking with a professional therapist, or at least unburdening to a wise and trusted friend or Spiritual Director. There are always times in our lives when we may need guidance getting started on a new path or to do an occasional "sanity check" when we may become so deeply entrenched in what is happening in our world that we can't see clearly. However, for the vast majority of those people confronting the daily challenges or vicissitudes of life, a clear understanding and plan of action is sufficient for guiding them through some, if not most, of the murky waters that continually appear from time to time during our lives. But ultimately, life is a process without end, and we cannot always have a therapist at hand to guide us through all the changes, challenges and transitions it brings. Nor would it be emotionally healthy to do so. We need to learn how to be, in most situations, our own healer and therapist; that is the way to self-actualization and is the ultimate road to individuation. All good therapists know that if they are successful with a client, they have worked themselves out of a job. While we might have to go to four different therapists to attain these four types of healing, because often therapies are linear and one basic therapeutic approach is preferred or used more often, we can walk ourselves through these four steps quite simply during many of the challenges to be faced. The more we use these steps in resolving everyday issues, the more effective we will be in handling the larger issues of life. Developing a habit of self-observation and a plan of action makes steering the course of our soul's growth easier, richer and more rewarding and ends in positive results, such as freedom and peace. Those are the qualities that have only been dreamed of during the times when we were evolving unconsciously and we were unaware that we could be co-creative partners with the Divine Mind.

While the four qualities in the healthy productive people that I talked about at the beginning of the chapter seemed to have, for most of them, evolved naturally or as the result of good role models when they were children, they quickly admitted that they apply these four basic principles/processes to almost every major issue in their lives. Often they are applied automatically, yet all four elements are always present to some degree in their final resolution. Others of us have learned to consciously apply these same processes, bit by bit, as we've read, meditated and learned from one teacher after another through the years. And while I suspect such learning will always be somewhat cumulative, we may be able to hasten our progress by seeing these four steps as parts of a whole larger process. It's a model that could benefit all people, and particularly the clients of most helping professions.

People who grew up in difficult times, during the Great Depression, the World Wars, etc., watched neighbors and parents employ some of these same processes on a daily basis. There were few entitlement programs and few social services, and everyone was having a difficult time surviving. This made it nearly impossible to rely on family or community generosity except where cooperation and mutual support were employed for the benefit of all. During that time period, these skills weren't normally labeled in psychological or spiritual terms; they were just plain basic survival skills and were often based on some type of faith. However, learning to survive made room for creativity and self-reliance, and ultimately, self-esteem came from knowing that even when life was tough, they could manage to find a path around the obstacles. How empowering. We need to model this confidence for our own children; what better legacy could we leave them?

Using processes which include both inner healing (right brain) and taking action (left brain) seems essential to healing. I have observed people who have spent years in therapy working solely on their inner processes, and who have employed all sorts of spiritual insights or platitudes and, yet, many of these individuals are still not able to live healthy lives. After several years they are still screaming, weeping and blaming. They remain immobilized as they view their victimhood.

While these inner processes are good, when they are used singulary without taking responsible action, they are often much less effective. When both inner synthesis and outer action are utilized together, they are potent agents of healing. Emoting is helpful, synthesizing and forgiving the actor while retaining a clear sense that the act was not acceptable, is essential, but also refusing to remain a victim of the past by taking responsible action to alter what needs to be changed now, becomes a must if one wishes to move forward and live a centered and happy life.

On the other hand, there are therapies and programs that stress only the outer processes and people are still, figuratively, left to "bleed and die" internally, or they continue to behave in unproductive ways. My friend Dorothy, once told me before she died, that after five years of psychotherapy she knew almost everything there was to know about herself but found nothing to "fill the inner void." Eventually, in the late 1960's, she found her spiritual path which employed inner healing meditations and it was at that point, in combination with her outer changes, she begin to find healing and a new wholeness.

Another clear case I read about told of a woman who went to her local women's shelter so battered that she had to remain hospitalized for several days. Her abuser was sent to prison. When the woman was released from the hospital, she began to get her life back in order. She went back to school and received her General Equivalency Diploma, (GED) found a good job and looked like she had made great progress. However, the day the abuser was released from prison the woman married him, they subsequently robbed a bank, and she ended up being incarcerated. We can only guess, but if she had received some intensive inner healing through psycho-synthesis, visualization, gestalt, dreams, journaling, etc. in addition to the outer life changes, perhaps there might have been a different outcome.

It is a strange paradox. We *do* need to express feelings, we do need to grieve, and we do need to grieve to the end of our grief when it finally "lets us go." However, we also need to live our lives as well. We deserve times of pleasure, happiness and well-being even around and outside our grief. Whatever our loss, there comes a point where we need to take charge of our lives, and while our grief and emotional processes are a part of life, it is much healthier when we come to realize that it is not *all* of our life, and we are no longer willing to allow it to consume us and leave us bitter and sad forever. Many people are finding that using a combination of both the inner and outer processes has assured them of a more successful outcome, and at times, that outcome is quite dramatic. Buddha felt that *"enlightenment"* is the middle way, the path between opposite extremes.

Ken Wilbur, in his book: *One Taste,* maintains that since we range from matter to body to mind to soul to spirit, we need to exercise all those levels by incorporating a practice from each level into our daily practices. Each level of practice enhances the other levels of our being, and there are many, many practices at each level from which one may make a choice. We hear a great deal about confluent education: the process of getting mind and emotions flowing together. Getting the body, mind, soul and spirit flowing and growing together is an integral approach that pays big dividends.

Summary

It seems that people who live relatively healthy and balanced lives, are those individuals who are able, consciously or unconsciously, to process the events in their lives through these four major channels and strike a balance between the inner and outer journeys. Even as a river has an inlet and an outlet to remain fresh, so humans must employ both introspection and action to stay vibrantly alive and healthy. In earlier decades we dealt so much with rational left brain psychological techniques that we often did not honor feelings. Then we moved to the opposite extreme and began dealing with feelings to such a degree that we often negated the value of taking action. Neither empirical data nor information from the affective domain is complete within itself. It is only half a picture when looked at in isolation from the other; wisdom dictates that we must be informed and use processes from both arenas to obtain optimal results. The four quadrant process is cumulative and, like most practices, increases in value and effectiveness with practice.

CHAPTER TWO

Clarifying Values

We all seek meaning and love through our
Work and the relationships we establish.
-Ione Jenson

We are now beginning to hear the phrase: *"conscious evolution."* Things are always changing and evolving; it is the very nature of *Nature* to transcend itself. However, up to this point in history, evolution has taken place without the conscious participation of most human beings. During the last half of the 20th century we began seeing larger and larger numbers of people growing into an awareness of just how they could influence and participate in the process. Throughout recorded history there have been the great Avatars, along with meta-physicians and mystics, who understood the principles and dynamics of the way things worked, but their numbers were limited. Today, large masses of humankind are beginning to understand that *"intention creates materiality."* Our very thoughts and actions are co-creative with the larger universal forces. We do have a great influence on how the world evolves, and more and more people are expanding their value systems to include valuing and embracing the world's diversity and our interdependence as we grow into a global community. We are being called to a new awareness as we move closer to becoming a *Universal Humanity*. This calls for a reexamination of our individual and collective lives.

One of the necessary steps for living an examined life is to determine our basic values. In his bestselling book: *The Seven Habits of Highly Effective People*, Stephen Covey dwells extensively on this point, and I would highly recommend reading his book for deeper insight into that process. However, most of us, with a little introspection, can determine some of the values we hold most dear. Many of these values may come from childhood and cultural programming, and we may want to spend some time determining whether they are really our values or just a programmed response to how we think we "should" behave or think. Still, other values we hold and may not act on as consistently as we'd like, are values that resonate deeply. (Ex: the value of unconditional love.) However, until we literally define and write down what it is we value, it is impossible to make any concerted effort to live those values in any kind of consistent manner. To define what we truly value may take quite a period of time, so don't be in a hurry to complete your list. It may take months, or even a year or two, to think through and write and rewrite your statement of values to your complete satisfaction. Even then, it is always a good idea to review it from time to time and revise it to reflect your expanding experience and to incorporate your changing viewpoints or goals.

To help you begin to sort and define your basic values, you might begin by looking at the following suggestions:

➢ As you think in terms of what you value, it is a good idea to think about the qualities you admire in other people. What you admire in others is a positive reflection of what you deeply value and what you would like to emulate. So a good place to begin is to jot down all the positive qualities you see in other people.

➢ Take time now to reflect on your own positive strengths and abilities. What is it you do well and what attitudes might others find admirable in you? Write down your response to these reflections about yourself.

> ➢ Another question might be: "If you had unlimited funds, what might you choose to do with your life?" Take a moment to write down the answers to this question.
> ➢ Move on by asking: "If I could create the finest planet, filled with the finest people I can imagine, what would that society and environment be like? What are the values I would like to have everyone in our world espouse?" Write down your responses.
> ➢ Ask: "If I were writing my own eulogy, what would I like to be able to say about myself?" Take some time and write it down.
> ➢ Consider this question: "If the people in my life, family, friends, coworkers, were writing my eulogy, what would I like them to say they thought I valued most?" Add this to your statement.
> ➢ If you were given just one year to live, how would you spend it?
> ➢ If after doing these exercises to assess your personal system of values, you still feel you need a little more guidance, *The Family Virtues Guide* by Linda Kavelin Popov will give you a more comprehensive look at many common values. You may peruse it and find which of those virtues listed resonate. I found it extremely helpful in aiding me in my quest to fully develop my own list.

As parents and grandparents, we need to begin helping our children develop values while they are very young, and we need to model for them a life lived in accordance with personal integrity.

All of these things we've just considered and written down will reflect for us some of our basic values. As I took myself through these steps again, not too long ago, I discovered one of my personal values comes from my childhood and is one that I feel is well worth keeping. That value is the knowledge that the world does not "owe me a living," but with honesty, integrity and the willingness to apply effort (work) there's not much I can't have or do within reason. We may not have had much in the way of material goods during my childhood, yet we always had all we needed, a few extras, and a little left over to share with someone else who had an unmet need. My mother was a careful manager of the family funds and could, as my grandmother used to say: "squeeze a nickel until the buffalo screams." (That gives a clue to the time frame I'm speaking about!) My sisters and I, from a very young age, also worked at whatever odd jobs we could find. However, I never remember us envying or resenting what other people had. If we felt we would like something someone else had, we knew that we could have it. We could work for it, save for it, or postpone it until we were older, but we always knew that if we valued it enough, someday, however far into the future, we could have it if it remained a high enough priority in our lives. Therefore, we never felt hopeless. We always felt that someday we could find a way to manage it. That's why I found it necessary to revise the way I executed one of my earlier values. One of those values is generosity, and several years ago I was an avid supporter of massive entitlement programs. However, with expanding wisdom and experience, I've come to see how oftentimes these programs, while originally intended to help, have actually often dis-empowered the recipients instead. I now find that while I still maintain the basic value of generosity, I'm opposed to blanket entitlement programs and have come to eye many of these programs with increasing trepidation. Seldom do they empower people to take control of their lives, but on the contrary, they tend to keep people pigeonholed in their self-made boxes. Saving money in the short term is not my goal, but creating programs of empowerment *is* what I value.

So if I truly believe in what I have written on my statement of basic values such as self-sufficiency, independence, and empowerment, I will also value those same things for others as well. I will refuse to allow myself to fall into feeling victimized, and I will not allow others to try to convince me that I am. I will state my convictions concisely and clearly should anyone try to make me out to be a victim or try to convince me of their own victim hood. However, I will continue to honor generosity, and I will continue to give freely but in a different way. Most of the gifts I give will each pass through the test of empowerment. I will ask myself the question: "Can this be given in such a way as to empower the person to be more responsible for their own well-being, to help them raise their own self-esteem or to aid them in being at least a little more in charge of their own lives and needs?"

13

There will be some cases, of course, where the need is so immediate, pressing or without possibility for empowerment that those questions will not be valid and some action becomes a necessity. However, a significant amout of giving does qualify for the empowerment test, and I will try to use my resources in the most positive and helpful way possible. I value doing what I can to increase the number of empowered people on our planet.

We can, and certainly should, help people out of tight places and catastrophic events in their lives, but a large share of society's effort would be better served if more time was spent on empowering people by teaching them to value independence, resourcefulness and personal responsibility. I know the argument will be: "But what of people in ghettos, people who have handicaps, etc?" I believe we must see there are laws guaranteeing equal rights, non-discrimination and provide good and equal educational opportunities, all while teaching the values of independence, resourcefulness and responsibility. Then, let's make certain there are ample opportunities for individuals to contribute to their own well-being and to the over-all good of their community. That concept will probably cost no more than entitlements, and with any luck, will soon produce a force of workers that will enhance the quality of life for themselves and others.

Our *Values* may be as expansive as wanting to learn to love unconditionally or to have unfailing trust in God. We may aspire to journey through our entire lifetime with a sincere and unflappable faith in Divine Order or Creative Intelligence. On the other hand, our goal may be as specific as wanting to get a college degree. Some of the larger values that we may hold are things such as: freedom to flow with inner guidance, spirituality, honesty, financial independence, time for fun, or to be: spontaneous, responsible, non-judgmental, non-prejudiced, compassionate, always learning, a contributor to the planet and humanity, etc. Many shorter term values include things such as: an education, one's own place, a car, satisfying relationships or job, travel, and so on. The list is ad infinitum and will reflect the differing values of those who make them.

Some of our values may change or need revision as we grow older, wiser, or both. Certainly the more life experience I've had and the more new information that has come to me, the more I have found that it has been necessary for me to change my perspective about some of my earlier values, or at least, the form in which I execute those values. And then again, certain values may never change nor need to be altered. They are unwavering and are likely to be our most expansive and deepest values. They are the ones which will probably remain constant and grow even more important with time.

However, some of our more specific values will probably change, or they may grow into a more expansive form. In the case of getting a college degree/s, we may accomplish that and turn it into a greater value by expressing the desire to always remain a learner and student of life itself. Some of the values we may feel deeply important at age 20, no longer seem desirable to us as we learn and grow and deepen our belief system. Some of these values may have been centered in earlier religious indoctrination. As we grow into a greater spiritual awareness, we might see that those original values were exclusive and are now dichotomous to some of our most important and basic values such as a non-judgmental acceptance of our fellow human beings and an ability to honor and embrace diversity. Under these circumstances, our basic values may expand or they may change altogether. As stated earlier, it is good to not only write down our basic values but to review them often, or at least annually and make any additions or changes that reflect our personal growth during the past twelve months, for we are an ever changing process.

Summary

We need to release both our crisis oriented and victim mentalities and work on integrating our lives physically, psychologically, mentally and spiritually. Defining our values is the essence of this quadrant. For without knowing what we value, it's impossible to create and maintain a healthy life. The clearer we are about our values, and the clearer we are in communicating those values to other people, the less apt we are to find ourselves in unhealthy and frustrating situations. And when each of us knows exactly where another person's values lie, the easier it is for us to respect them and work toward the highest good of all involved.

Action Steps

Get a three ring notebook so you can add and subtract pages as needed. Start by setting aside the time to sit quietly and very thoughtfully answer the seven questions at the beginning of the chapter. Give each question its own page whether you fill it up or not.

- ➤ Check over each page and jot down on that page just which of those things listed you accept as a personal value for your own life.
- ➤ Take a clean sheet of paper and list each value until you have a list that states your basic system of values; this is the standard you want to live by. Save.
- ➤ If further clarification is needed, you may choose to read one of the books listed in the Recommended Reading List at the back of the book.

CHAPTER THREE

Action: Modifying Behavior

Inner power comes from knowing we can
Change the things that aren't working in our lives.
-Ione Jenson

In this quadrant, it's essential to remember that once our values are defined, all our choices need to support those values. The choices we make will either enhance or deflect from our values and goals. We need to honestly assess just where our daily lives and actions reflect our values and where they do not. One of the most powerful ways to assess how our lives align with our basic value system, is to spend a few moments each evening looking back over the day. In this retrospective review, look at the days events and how you handled them; here you can see how closely your actions were in line with your stated values. It's not productive to chastise yourself for the places you missed, but as an objective observer, gently go over it and choose a different way to respond the next time. Life invariably offers us the same lessons and opportunities again and again until we've mastered them. In those places where we are genuinely living out what we hold dear, we can move forward and continue to grow and live more closely aligned with ourselves.

In those areas where our day-to-day life fails to align with what we have stated as a value, we need to take some concrete *ACTION* steps that will lead us to discover what may be blocking us from living what we value. Only then will we begin to find permanent solutions for the issues we face. These may necessarily be very small steps in the beginning, particularly if the challenge we face seems overwhelming, but we need to make some forward movement by taking some positive action toward resolution. We also need to look at what we value, and then observe where we spend our time and how we live our lives in order to bring these two facets into alignment. If we desire, for example, to live in a clean environment, if we want our planetary evolution to move toward peace at all levels, if we desire not to be abused by others, we must begin with self-responsibility. We must begin doing our part in creating a clean environment, we must live our lives as peaceful, loving, giving individuals, and we must be certain that we take personal responsibility never to abuse others; it all begins with us. We must develop "response-ability" for living our daily lives in integrity and in alignment with what we value.

As we come to understand the basic values we want to embody in our life, it then becomes necessary to begin to take the following steps:

➢ Develop and draw healthy boundaries in order to live congruently with our values.
➢ Look at every situation and see it realistically and honestly.
➢ Evaluate how we might need to modify our behavior, sometimes through contracts with ourselves, in order to make our life work in a more productive way.
➢ Learn how to assertively communicate our values and our boundaries to others.

These four steps in the *ACTION* quadrant will aid us significantly in taking charge of our life and in moving us forward toward constructive solutions as well as toward wholeness and healing.

It is a fact that even while we may be engulfed with emotions, we can also use that pain to change our lives. Life is full of paradoxes. We do need to allow ourselves to grieve to the bottom of the grief, but it is also possible to get into a victim mentality until our grief becomes a bottomless pit, never to be satisfied. It is definitely possible to become addicted to the drama or to be addicted to the euphoria of crisis; we all know people who are always in the midst of a crisis, and if not, they are busy creating one. A close friend once confided that she used to create drama and crisis in her life as a way of feeling alive. Otherwise, if she was not dealing with catastrophes, she felt dead inside and bored with life.

There are always those people who would rather live with pain and anxiety than take some of the small painstaking steps that will lead them to the solution. These are the people with what I call a "case of the yah-buts." No matter what steps they might take to move out of their drama, they always have an excuse for not doing so. If someone suggests that there might be some alternatives after listening to their lengthy complaints, they say: "Yah, but I can't do that because," and then go on to give numerous excuses as to why any suggested course of action will not work. Not that they have necessarily tried it, but they do not want to make any effort or take any responsibility for improving their own situation. Stuart Wilde asserts in *Whispering Winds of Change*: "Each year more victims will join the ranks because being a victim is easier than taking responsibility or generating energy. You can blame your problem or your lack of concerted disciplined action on others."

There are people envious of what others have or achieve, and yet, they aren't willing to take the action required to reach those same goals for themselves. A friend once told me that I was lucky because I had a savings account. Luck had little to do with it; I made a deposit each payday. And I was often willing to do without many luxuries in order to have a little reserved for future use, while she on the other hand, spent everything she earned and then charged her credit cards to the maximum. She earned more money than I did, but the major difference between us was the will to save and the action necessary to make it happen.

Before she died my eldest sister confided, after many years, that she had always been jealous of me because I'd had an opportunity to get a college degree while she had been denied that luxury. After hearing her complain about this on several separate occasions, I finally reminded her of the reality of our situations. Although our parents had not been able to send us through college, I chose to attend a local college and literally worked at any and all available jobs in order to put myself through the first two years. Six years after I married, my husband, child and I had done without many material comforts in order for me to take classes which eventually culminated in a college degree. Because money was so scarce back then, I took one, two or three classes as money and time allowed. I went evenings, summers, and during the day when I could manage it. A few semesters or summers there wasn't enough money for a class so I sat it out and continued to save for the next session. Three and a half years later, I finally finished those final credits and received my degree. I had driven over 80 miles round trip to attend classes, and because we were a one car family, I often had my husband drop me off at his parent's house on his way to work where it was then necessary for me to transfer on three different buses in order to reach the University. I made the return trip by the same conveyances in which I had arrived, often after my last class ended at 10 p.m.

My sister, who during those same years lived right in a university town and had easy access to classes, had never taken advantage of a single one. I reminded her of these facts and that the difference between us had been one of will and determination to take action. I had decided that completing my education was my way to financial freedom and would take care of the financial challenges facing my family. There was no luck involved, only the fact that I made the decision to go to college and she didn't. With that discussion, she was faced with confronting the truth, and she never discussed my "luck" or her "jealousy" about my education (or her lack of one) again.

When we put forth energy and action, we are preparing for the best life has to offer; luck has little to do with our good fortune. Most instances of synchronicity or serendipity are the result of the efforts we make to visualize, conceptualize and move forward with heart and will. Self-actualizing people have confidence in their abilities, trust their intuitive nature and see challenges as opportunities to prove their mettle. According to David G. Meyers who is the author of: *The Pursuit of Happiness*, (William Morrow, 1992) "People who have an internal locus of control, those who believe they choose their own destiny, typically achieve more, cope better with stress, and live more happily than those who feel their directions are determined by outside forces."

Facing Reality

If we are going to attain wholeness and learn effective processes for dealing with life, it is absolutely essential to face the reality of any given situation and honestly confront the issue. Once this has been accomplished, we are then in a position to observe both the drawbacks and the potential solutions. From this position, we can determine some viable ways to take action and implement change.

In her book: *Choosing Truth: Living an Authentic Life,* Harriette Cole calls us to decide what we believe and to be true to our values even in a morally confused world. In other words, we have to honestly face the reality of our own life and then govern our individual behavior according to what we value. The manner in which we expect and desire others to behave is a clarion call for us to first make those actions a firm part of our daily response in all situations.

As important as our past history may be, and as directly as it may impact the present and need healing work, we still must squarely face the current challenges and be willing to take constructive action. It's also important to realize that some of the difficult situations in which we find ourselves may be related to personality differences and not dysfunction per se. Each person will have their own value system, and while many values may be the same, there are bound to be differences in what people feel is important. If you live with an avid gardener and they are unhappy if you do not share the work they have lined up, it is good to recognize that you may not have to "dig into" underlying causes of resistance; you merely have to honor how each person chooses to spend their time and energy.

On the other hand, there will be times when such incidents are really power and control issues, and one needs to take a look at the insecurities or fears that impel one to desire control over another. However, even when there are reasons that relate to earlier experiences or memories and which, surely, need to be worked through, it is still necessary to face the reality of the situation and take action. I may or may not be able to help the other person explore their inner need for control over my behavior, but I can realistically face the fact that gardening is not my way of self-expression, and I can lovingly make it clear that I do not choose to spend my time and energy in that pursuit.

Here is another example of the personality differences that might exist between people. If you were an only child and grew up enjoying large spaces of solitude, and as an adult you still require periods of time alone, you may simply need to honor that facet of your personality. Should you happen to live with someone from a large and involved brood of children who likes constant background noise, you're going to need to assess the situation as accurately as possible and then take constructive action.

Perhaps, if your partner (or roommate) is willing, the two of you can sit down and work out a win/win solution and enable each of you to find ways to honor your individual needs. If that is not possible, then you may have to look realistically at your need for quiet time and how you can attain time alone. You may need to take a day each week to go off by yourself, you may need to have a room that is yours and that is not accessible to other family members, or you may need to consider other living arrangements, particularly if you are not in a marital situation or don't have children.

Under these circumstances, taking into account the reasons behind each person's preference is essential for understanding and comfortable compromise. However, it may or may not necessarily mean either person needs inner healing unless, of course, one is using noise to distract oneself from inner pain, or using silence as an avoidance technique, but it might just be a signal for balancing and accommodating the personal needs of all concerned.

William Glasser in his book: *Reality Therapy*, (1965, Harper and Row) tells about psychotic patients in the Veterans Neuropsychiatric Hospital in West Los Angeles, some of whom had been there for two or more decades. The patients on the closed ward numbered fifty and were the most difficult and resistant to treatment. When Reality Therapy was introduced on the ward, the new staff was carefully instructed not to accept the situation as hopeless, and that each patient could do better "if they can be helped to help themselves, they will slowly but surely act more responsibly."

Bit by bit these formerly incapacitated men were expected to take responsibility for their basic functions such as eating, brushing their teeth, shaving, bathing, etc. Even when they were in cuffs, they were expected to take some responsibility for their personal care even when it was awkward to do so. Carefully, and step by step, they were led toward increasing levels of functioning until they were able to first move into the semi-open ward, then to the open ward, to being permitted to take outside excursions first with family and then on their own. Eventually, they moved out to live with family, a foster home or in an apartment where they retained the support of the program but were primarily dependent upon themselves. Glasser contends that by taking steadily increasing responsibility, the patients began to gain both self-respect and self-worth. If this process can create functioning human beings from psychotic men in strait jackets, shouldn't we be able to understand the value of self-responsibility and use the concept to help ourselves and to help others to do likewise?

Taking action is very frequently a necessary component which aids the inner healing processes which will be discussed more fully in the third quadrant. Frequently people come and want to work with their inner issues, which is wonderful, but then are reluctant to take any outside action steps that reinforce the inner work they have been doing. I well remember a woman who was experiencing a physical challenge, and when we looked at possible body-mind connections several loomed before her. However, when we began to address the need for changes in her life to correct the underlying stress that was aggravating her physical condition, it terrified her. She was so frightened of "rocking the boat" in her outside world, she begged: "Can't we just work with helping me heal within so I will be able to accept these outer things and not be stressed about them?" Since the "outside things" constituted very real abuse issues, learning to accept them more than she already had been trying to do, would have been detrimental to her body. Eventually she did see the connection and began making positive, even though small, steps in those outer circumstances that were creating such stress in her life and body. Unfortunately, often people are not willing to take constructive action regardless of how miserable they know their life to be.

The basis of Reality Therapy is simple. It is based on the premise that everyone needing psychiatric treatment, regardless of the symptoms, suffers from one basic inadequacy, they are unable to fill their basic needs. The essential psychological needs are to love and be loved and to feel worthwhile to oneself and others. Glasser does not deny the impact of the past. However, he does feel that we must not allow that to keep us from learning how to fulfill our needs in the present. My premise is that facing reality in any given situation and taking responsibility for ourselves is one essential component for healing, and when we couple that with the other three quadrants we are exploring in this book, we have both short and long term results with each process complimenting and reinforcing the others.

Over and over again, each of us must ultimately face whether or not we are willing to walk the path of personal responsibility in order to fulfill our needs and to do so without depriving others of the opportunity to fulfill theirs. Facing reality can be harsh, it can be painful, and it usually calls for change, often times, radical change. We must decide time and again during our lifetime whether or not we are going to face issues with a willingness to take the risk and bear the temporary pain of creating a more preferable environment in which to live and grow, or whether we are going to choose to stay and live with the continued pain and conflict of the present situation.

Modifying Behavior

Most of the time, if we choose the path of personal responsibility, we find that, in reality, the process of change may come slowly and we may need to take thoughtful action in small palatable pieces. As we bit by bit begin to modify our behavior to align with our deepest values and desired goals, we learn the value of taking manageable steps. It's not realistic to think that we can change everything overnight, but over time, we will become more and more empowered as we take increasing responsibility toward creating the necessary changes to live a happier, healthier and more productive life.

Underlying a great deal of our immobility lies the lack of will/energy/ambition to take responsibility for changing things. I have to honestly admit that many times when I have portrayed (or observed others portraying) helplessness, it's simply been a lack of personal ambition and a harboring of hope that somebody would come along and do it for me. When I have seemed or even felt the most helpless, under it all, I have also known there were certain actions I could take and behaviors I could modify that would change the situation. I just didn't have the will or ambition to do them, especially if I could get someone else to do it for me.

I remember as a young farm wife waiting for the men to paper the walls of our old farmhouse. It was during a busy time, and after sitting in the middle of the mess for weeks on end grumbling, complaining, crying and feeling like a victim, I finally said to myself, "You've never wallpapered a room in your life, however, you have observed how it's done. You also have seen your older friend, Lucille Pelzer, plaster, wallpaper and undertake all kinds of similar projects, and you've always admired her greatly. Get in there and just try one strip and see if you can do it." I measured carefully and tentatively cut one strip. I placed it face down on the wallpapering table (made of sawhorses and wooden planks) mixed up some wheat paste according to package directions (I read and followed cookbook recipes all the time, what is so different?) and took the paste brush I had been watching the men use. I spread the paste over the back of the wallpaper and then lifted it to the wall and carefully placed it on the wall, being careful to match the pattern with the previous strip already on the wall. I picked up the dry brush and brushed the paper firmly in place, just as I had watched Lucille and the guys do. I then took the cutting tool and trimmed the paper off level with the ceiling and tightly against the mop board near the floor. Eureka! It looked fine. I decided to try another strip and repeated the performance. Elated with the results, I cut, pasted, pressed into place on the wall and trimmed strip after strip until the entire room was finished. The next day I set out to do the remaining room and had completed it by evening's end. Weeks of playing the victim hadn't accomplished the job, however, two days of accepting the responsibility for taking action finished the task, and I took great pride in knowing I would never again be waiting for someone to paper my walls unless I chose to do so.

Today, I still occasionally observe myself being tempted to ask someone how to do something and then willingly allow them to take it and do it for me instead of following their instructions and doing it myself so that the next time I'll know how it's done. Even after literally building a house, which my friend Masil and I did in 1981, I'd rather get someone else to put together a book shelf or desk for me than I would to do it myself. If I decide, however, that I'd rather not do something myself when I know that I'm perfectly capable of doing so, then that is a legitimate choice. But, I must also be willing to relax and realize I am not a victim no matter what twists and turns the project takes. There will be things we choose to hire done because it is something we've not chosen to do, or do not choose to gain the expertise in learning to do. If I choose to hire something done, then I must take responsibility for hiring the best person for the job, and make certain I have a contract stating specifics. Human creatures that we are, it seems so much easier sometimes to rely on, or blame, something or someone outside ourselves. A friend once mused: "It was so much easier when I believed it was being done unto me."

Understanding my own tendencies to want others to take responsibilities I don't like to carry, I also understand manipulations. As I diligently watch for and immediately attempt to eradicate any of my own attempts at manipulation, I am also astutely aware when another person attempts to "play games" or manipulate me. If someone asks me for help with a task because I have tackled so many varied projects, and I know it's something they can very well do or learn to do themselves, I begin by telling them that I will be happy to empower them by showing them how to do it. Then step-by-step I stand by and allow them to master the project as I instruct when needed. I'm not easy to manipulate anymore, because once you are consciously aware of your own games, it's easy to see through them when another person is attempting to play them.

These are the rewards of self-observation and self-understanding. I believe I'm not too different than most people; we often know better, we just don't do better. However, if we get tired enough of the crisis, we will often move forward. As my grandmother used to say: "When you get your belly full of it, maybe you'll do something about it!"

Several years ago, there was an article about a nurse who wanted a new house. Though divorced, single parenting and struggling financially, she sat down and made out a list of her options. She began to think in terms of "possible" instead of "impossible." She explored every option on her list, and when one banker turned down her request for a loan, she went to another one. She finally found a banker willing to work with her limited resources and who appreciated her determination and will to make it happen. She cut costs by doing much of the work herself. She cut trees, hauled dirt and tarred the foundation. She painted, caulked, sanded and plastered. In short, she spent hundreds of back breaking hours in doing and learning how to complete her home. Out of this experience she has gained one priceless insight, she now knows that if she wants something badly enough, she can do it.

This is, I think, one of the strengths of Habitat for Humanity. While it is willing to recognize that people need a helping hand and may not be able to gather all the resources necessary to build themselves a home, it does require commitment and action on the part of its recipients. They must help get local donations as well as put in a minimum number of hours in physical labor completing the house. In return for their direct involvement and willingness to help in attaining a home for themselves, they get an interest free loan with a small repayment plan and a nice house to live in. These are a few of the ways in which we can encourage individuals to take increasing responsibility for fulfilling their needs and yet lend enough of a helping hand to aid them in bringing it to fruition.

So frequently it is not the events of our lives that affect what happens to us, but rather it is our interpretation of those events that limit us. George Bernard Shaw once said: "The people who get on in this world look for the circumstances they want. If they don't find them, they make them." How do we do that? That is what this book is all about. If you will take a moment and ask yourself these questions, you will have some surprising answers.

> ➢ If you were given a year to live, what would you choose to do with your last year? Think about it for a moment. Since fear so often stops us from taking risks, and in this question since death is inevitable, most people can move past the fear. Steven Levine, author and teacher who has worked and written extensively about death and dying, refers to this process of living as though you were dying, as a race against death to complete your birth, to fulfill your heart's (soul's) destiny.
> ➢ If money were no object, what would you do with your life? Don't be afraid to dream BIG. Become proactive and choose to respond based on what you value, rather than on your feelings or the fear of what others may think.

More likely than not, we allow genetics, past programming and childhood experiences, and our outer environment (job, boss, spouse, finances, etc.) to determine what we do, or what we are afraid to do. Under those circumstances we feel victimized and at the disposal of all things outside ourselves. To become proactive means we see all the outside factors, but we move beyond them and determine our own life and course of action. This brings to mind again Victor Frankl, the Jewish political prisoner during WWII who has written such classics as: *"Man's Search for Meaning"* and *"From Psychotherapy to Logo Therapy."* He talks about *the last ultimate freedom* and says that liberty is external; freedom is internal.

Finally, and worth noting, are the studies that have proven that one of the greatest factors, not only in peace and happiness but also in longevity, is *resilience*. Resiliency and the ability to integrate changes, challenges and transitions in a healthy way and to get through, move past and thrive after life has thrown you an unexpected "curve ball," is the single most important attribute you can develop and acquire. The very events we may view as trials, trauma, and tribulations can be the impetus (evolutionary drivers) that move us to transcend to the next upward level of our personal, and sometimes, cultural and collective evolution.

Being adept at accepting change, meeting challenges creatively, and embracing the transitions and phases of this journey called *Life*, are the life blood of what has made our country a great nation. The skill of being resilient and able to embrace and overcome challenges has definitely been a vital part of human history or we would not have continued to exist and evolve as a humanity. Our major choices are: to confront things unconsciously and bumble through complaining and feeling victimized, or, face all events consciously, courageously and with a sense of confidence and connection to a Divine source or Creative energy that moves us forward.

Resiliency can be learned, and it can certainly be fostered in our children. Educational practices must change and move to include opportunities within the educational setting that allow children to grow in their ability to acquire good decision-making skills, to understand the natural consequences of the choices they make, and to take responsibility for what they do and say. Problem solving techniques, peacemaking strategies, and resilience are only a few of the major skills that will be required of them in the 21st century and beyond.

During the summers of 2000 and 2001, I was involved in setting up and teaching at Camp Indigo in Coeur d'Alene, Idaho. During that time, I taught in the "I Care Room" and was reminded once again of the intrinsic value of early childhood education and how quickly children pick up and utilize concepts when they are modeled and taught in a loving and respectful context. We used the materials of Foster Cline and Jim Fey on parenting and teaching with *Love and Logic*, as well as the powerful materials from *The Peace Education Foundation*. The ideas contained in Linda Popov's book: *The Family Virtues Guide* may also be helpful. Not only are these materials solid instructional modalities for children through High School, but adults will profit from reading and applying them to their own lives as well. I can see dynamic nuclear family units developing from parents willing to utilize these concepts within their family structures. I am equally certain these same principles have the potential for being far broader and greater than just in individual lives and individual families. However, the changes must first occur with individuals before we can hope for a broader context. I love being an involved grandparent, so for those who wish to do *conscious* grand parenting, Cline and Fey have written a wise guide to: *Grand Parenting with Love and Logic*.

In 2002, I helped develop the concept of School Indigo which operated, privately, in Coeur d'Alene. School Indigo had an integrated curriculum and a program on the principles I have just described. However, Judie Brown who was the force behind the school, and the financial backer, became ill and died about six years after its opening. The school could not, financially, survive the loss. However, many children were the recipients of a rich educational experience during those six years.

Learning to Set Boundaries

As we establish just what we value and how we need to modify our behavior in order to live out those values, it becomes essential to learn how to begin setting firm and healthy boundaries. These boundaries will need to be set both on our own behaviors and on the behaviors we will or will not tolerate from others.

For instance, if we are to value ourselves, and it is certainly to be hoped that is one universal value common to everyone, we will need to set some firm boundaries around what we will and will not allow others to do to us. If we value ourselves, we will not allow others to devalue us. We may listen to honest statements about how another person is affected by us and make a honest attempt to try working out win/win solutions that allow each person to hold on to their inner integrity. However, we will not allow anyone to abuse us physically or emotionally. Should that occur, we will state our position as powerfully and as non-abusively as possible, but will not continue to remain in situations where that takes place. If we need to take action by leaving the physical environment or disengaging ourselves from the relationship, we will take that step. We will have firm boundaries, to whatever extent necessary, to put an abrupt halt to any abuse. That is a firm and definite boundary around the value we place on ourselves.

I read an article in a newspaper concerning a woman who had been very abused by her husband, to the point of having a gun drawn on her, but who was asking the judge to remove the restraining order against him. The director of a local battered women's shelter made this statement: "We have to stop asking why she doesn't leave and ask why he thinks he can behave that way. Society should hold his feet to the fire!" The director's premise was that the woman had a "right" to try and make her marriage work; the man held the responsibility for being abusive.

Well, indeed he does need to be asked why he thinks he can behave abusively, and he does need to be accountable for his behavior, however, she too needs to be asked why she doesn't leave. We need to help women like this find value in themselves, and we need to encourage them to draw good healthy boundaries around what kind of behavior they will accept. The bottom line is simply this, as long as we are willing to accept abusive people into our lives and continue to support their power and control issues by accepting the abuse, we will most certainly continue to draw them into our lives. Valuing ourselves needs to be a high priority on anyone's list of values, for how can we truly value anyone else if we have little or no regard for ourselves. Others are most likely to respond to us with the same degree of regard that we have for ourselves. Water does, indeed, seek its own level.

We will, as faithful observers, often find our behavior and the behavior of those around us to be contrary to what we have determined to be some of our basic values. In discovering this truth, we will find we need to modify some of our actions if we are to be true to our values. For instance, if being a non-prejudiced person and living a life that accepts people for who they are is one of our values, then we must set some boundaries or limits on what we find acceptable or unacceptable. We will no longer participate in ethnic jokes that reduce other people to objects of scorn, nor will we participate in any activities that will exclude other people on the basis of race, gender, or lifestyle. We will not allow anything that takes place in our homes to demoralize or be harmful to others. These will be our boundaries and will be enforced as clearly as the "no smoking" rule that governs many of our homes.

Depending on how important we deem this particular value to be, we may take some additional or optional steps that modify our usual patterns even further. We may want to move to a new location or spend extended periods of time in more multi-cultural situations. Perhaps, we will choose to take part in some activities that promote equal rights, integration, equal opportunity or respect for diversity. We might take college courses in ethnic history or read the works of authors of other races to gain additional insight and understanding. We may use our talents as writers, artists, speakers, amid other things, to in some way extend understanding between people, or to make a place for open dialogue and conflict resolution to occur. There are any number of ways in which we can take constructive action to help enhance what we value and make the world, or some small piece of it, a little more accepting and a little more loving. So once we have our values in place, it becomes necessary to draw certain boundaries that uphold those values. It also strengthens our position if we take some positive action and modify some aspects of our lifestyle to accommodate the deeper expression of what it is that we value.

As mentioned in the quadrant on *VALUES*, what we hold as our basic values may be as expansive as wanting to learn to unfailingly trust in Process/God and journey through our entire lifetime with a sincere and unflappable faith in Divine Order, or they may be as specific as wanting to get a college degree. Either value will call for modifying our behavior and for determining some firm boundaries. In the case of the first value, we will have to place firm boundaries around a commitment to make time and space to deal consistently with our fears as they arise. We will also need to practice spiritual disciplines that enhance our connection to the Divine Force or to the Kingdom Within. We will have to set boundaries around anything that keeps us from having time to develop the habits that make learning to walk in faith and trust possible. In the latter instance of a specific value, such as aspiring to a college degree, we may have to modify spending habits in order to save for tuition, we may have to alter our social life to accommodate studying, and we may have to set firm boundaries around anything, like sales or parties which might sabotage our plan of action.

Communicating Values and Boundaries

Once we have determined at least some of our basic values and set up certain personal boundaries in our attempt to begin to live, as nearly as possible, up to that standard, we often find ourselves faced with the dilemma of how to communicate this effectively when the need arises.

Many times, of course, the boundaries affect no one else so the need for communicating them is eliminated. However, sometimes, even an inner boundary ends up affecting others to some degree so that communication does become necessary. If we determine that we are going to write, undisturbed, for four hours each day while living with other people, then we need to communicate our intent and our boundaries with them. For example, if we live alone, we can let the answering machine take our telephone calls and we can return them later. However, if others are living in the household and want to answer the phone each time it rings, then we must make it clear that we are not willing to be disrupted during the hours we have set aside for writing. They may either take a message and we will return the call, or they can ask the caller to try again after we've finished work for the day. Setting a boundary and communicating it clearly saves us from being disturbed or from getting angry at either the caller or the person who answered the phone. Since neither of those people are mind readers, they can't be expected to know our boundaries unless we have effectively communicated those boundaries to them.

Often we hesitate to set and communicate our boundaries because we fear conflict, especially if we feel the other person will not easily accept the boundary we have established. That, of course, is always possible. However, I have found that if I think it out carefully, have made every attempt to see that I'm being reasonable and not impinging on anyone else's freedom or boundary in the process, and then state my position clearly without hesitation or room for argument, most people will comply whether they like it or not. It's imperative to note that it is not necessary for others to approve of our boundary in order for us to hold firmly to it. In fact, often they may not approve and that may be exactly why we've had to set the boundary in the first place. If someone keeps barging in on our time of solitude, for example, we may have to communicate that this not acceptable. Of course, they are not going to like it and they will prefer that we always remain accessible. However, our boundary is reasonable, and if we hold to it regardless of their arguments, quietly but firmly asserting our need for times of positive solitude, they will eventually have to comply. If, on the other hand, my boundary does directly affect another person, such as using a room that is mutually shared for my time of solitude, then that person and I will need to sit down and negotiate a win/win situation and set some mutual boundaries on the time and usage of the shared space.

Learning to communicate about the values and boundaries we have set up for ourselves is a matter of deciding how we can best take care of ourselves and keep our personal integrity intact while respecting others and keeping their integrity intact as well. This is important in all types of relationships from the most causal to the most intimate. It was a revelation for me in the early 1970's when I took an Assertiveness Training class and learned the difference between assertiveness and aggressiveness. I think I had always used them interchangeably and thought there were only two ways of responding to my needs. One was to be angry and demand what I thought I needed or wanted, or the other way was to be passive, give in and save an argument. What a relief it was to discover that was not so. A viable third choice was available to me. I did not have to get angry, I did not have to make the other person wrong, but instead, I could assume the responsibility for what I thought or felt, assume the responsibility for my own happiness and for obtaining what I needed, and I could do all this without feeling unreasonable or guilty. Often the unreasonableness or guilt that I had previously felt when I set boundaries or took charge of getting what I needed, came from the aggressive attitude and behavior that I displayed in doing it. Once I learned that I could take the responsibility for getting what I needed without blaming the other person for not giving it to me, once I learned I did not have to be belligerent or nasty to assert myself, it became so much easier. If the other person responded angrily to a reasonable and calmly stated boundary, then I knew immediately the problem was their issue not mine.

Assertiveness and Beyond

Because assertiveness is so essential in the setting of and maintaining boundaries, I will elaborate a bit on this process. What is assertiveness all about? Assertiveness has been looked upon as a good tool for personal growth by both men and women. It has also been seen as an excuse to be obnoxious and pushy. Like many psychological tools, it does not present anything totally new; it is just another way to deal with personal relationship problems. It comes down to asking how we can take care of ourselves and keep our personal integrity, while at the same time, respecting others and their integrity. This is important in all relationships from the most casual to the most intimate.

The human relationship issue was addressed clearly and simply by Jesus when he said: "Do unto others as you would have them do unto you." This golden rule appears in some form in the religious texts and writings of all major religions; so if this is so clear, why don't we practice it as an entire human race? Even those who try to live by this beautiful maxim do not seem to be able to apply it consistently. Assertiveness is one avenue that aids us in the process of application, and it helps us love ourselves as well as our neighbors.

There are three basic behaviors that occur in our interactions with others. (1) Non-assertive = I am not ok/but you are OK, (2) Assertive = I am OK/you are OK, (3) Aggressive = I am OK/you are not OK. Each of us exhibits all these behaviors from time to time, but each of us also embodies one of these as our dominant approach to most conflicts. Often our reactions are the result of early events and learned behaviors. However, change is possible if we really want to begin to evolve consciously, and if we are willing to develop our capacity to listen to an inner objective observer, our higher self or our Divine counterpart. It has often been called "our conscience," which can be true, but don't confuse it with the inner judge who criticizes, chastises and "beats you up." The Divine Observer reminds us, without harsh judgment, that we may want to look at what we have done or said and correct our error.

Passive people are non-assertive and do not stand up for themselves, or they do it so ineffectively that their rights are violated anyway. Passive people generally have low self-esteem and are quite practiced in pushing down feelings or surrendering to another's demands, thus becoming long-suffering martyrs. A good example of this: A friend calls and wants to borrow money. You have a little extra put aside, but planned to go shopping for a new jacket. However, instead you give your friend the money and feel resentful.

Still another side of the passive person is termed "passive aggressive." This is the person who is too fearful to be outright aggressive, but who will find ways, often unconsciously, to express aggression in a less direct manner. An example of this behavior: Your spouse wants you do a task that you do not want to do, but you are un-willing to just say no. You promise to get the errand done before you come home from work, but then forget to stop before the store closes. A passive aggressive person can also be very consciously manipulative, getting what they want and need in underhanded ways.

The aggressive person usually also suffers from low self-esteem and has learned to bully and push others around. This behavior has often been rewarded because too many people have been afraid to challenge the aggression and have backed off and given the bully what s/he wanted. This one needs no further explanation for we all have seen this operate.

Obviously, these types of behavior detract from everyone's quality of life, and the more we indulge in these unproductive behaviors, the more miserable everyone becomes. These behaviors need to be dealt with, and we will be learning some ways this can happen in the next quadrant on *Inner Healing*.

The healthy, well-balanced and assertive person has excellent boundaries and acts in their own best interests, is able to take good care of themselves, and expresses honest needs, desires and feelings directly and clearly. All this is accomplished while respecting the rights of others - including and accepting the other's right to say no to requests. An example: The assertive person respects diversity and will speak in support of their own beliefs while, at the same time, listening carefully with an open mind to the other person's viewpoint.

There are a few tips that are helpful to remember when you are applying assertiveness:

➢ *Look* at the person as you speak.
➢ *Use body language* to communicate. Stand/sit erect. (Slumping, backing away, and nervous mannerisms have non-assertive messages.)

> ➤ *Listen* to the other person until you think you understand. Then repeat what you have heard to the other person's satisfaction.

> ➤ *Express feelings*, both positive and negative, but take responsibility for them. Ex: I am feeling angry because you didn't phone and tell me you would be late for dinner. Use "I" language, such as "I feel," never "you made me feel." Don't name call (you inconsiderate slob) and stick to specific behavior. Don't box someone in a corner with no way out.

> ➤ *Focus.* Stick to the point, repeat what you want. Don't be led into arguments.

> ➤ *Don't apologize for saying "no."* Some ways of saying no are: "No, I don't feel comfortable with that," or, "no, I can't do that." Or even just "no, I don't want to."

> ➤ *Kindness, empathy, and compassion* are components of *Assertiveness!*

> ➤ *State clearly what you will do.* Try not to spend time emphasizing what you won't do, but try to be positive about what you will do. Ex: If someone asks you to have dinner with them and you have other plans, you may tell them that you have other plans, but you would like to meet them for lunch on Tuesday. Or if you have been asked to do a favor for someone, you might reply that your schedule does not permit doing the favor they have asked, but that you will say a prayer for them.

The real advantages of becoming assertive are myriad. When the assertive person expresses boundaries, needs and desires, emotions are not pushed down and tensions are resolved immediately. The assertive person is free to become more joyful and spontaneous. At the same time, the assertive person knows that others have rights, needs and boundaries as well and respects those. Interactions and relationships have a much better opportunity to be richly textured and mutually satisfying when assertiveness and respect are the norm.

There may be times and situations when being non-assertive is appropriate and comes from a place of power not weakness. A good example of this: A close friend is having a bad day and wants to talk with you. You have plans to have a leisurely and quiet day by yourself, but your friend never asks anything from you and always gives so much, so you choose to lay your plans aside and spend time with her.

There are also a few risks one must be willing to take when becoming assertive. Rejection and ridicule may happen when we have to stand firm and even lovingly enforce our boundaries. The passive-aggressive person, caught in their fears and with an inability to have strong boundaries, may be envious or angry and may "back-bite spreading rumors or confidential information in an attempt to take revenge. When someone changes and becomes strong, it always changes the dynamics of relationships and may be threatening to the other person. The aggressive person may increase the demands and bullying in an all-out effort to get you back "under their domination and control." A passive partner may withdraw or become excessively afraid and apologetic.

There are some valid questions you may want to think about before taking an assertive stance:

➢ Is it appropriate?
➢ How important is the situation?
➢ How will I feel tomorrow if I am assertive today?
➢ How will I feel tomorrow if I am not assertive today?
➢ Am I prepared to deal with the consequences of being assertive?

Eventually, we must all learn to communicate our boundaries effectively in order to live up to the values we have determined to be the course we want to live by. And, even once we have set up healthy boundaries and communicated them effectively, we may find that we need to do so over and over again. Some people are cumulative learners and will not take our boundaries seriously unless we are unwavering over a period of time, and new situations and new people will require repetition as well. Setting boundaries and communicating our limits does get easier with practice, but we will always have to be a faithful observer of both ourselves and others in order to hold fast to the boundaries and values we hold.

Whenever we feel angry, hurt or depressed, we can be almost certain that we have failed to establish a good healthy boundary or else we have allowed our boundaries to become fuzzy or breached. A little introspection by asking ourselves the question: "What boundary is being breached?" will usually help clear up the reason. Then we can take the necessary steps to re-establish the boundary and assertively communicate where it is appropriate. Sometimes, the fear of conflict or the fear of being rejected or disliked is so strong that we will allow another to bend our boundary, and we will need to work with fears that may surface while reconnecting with our basic value and creating the limits that aid us in choosing to live in accordance with what we stand for.

At times, we will breach a boundary with ourselves, and it is just as necessary to check out our behavior in light of what we value and then reaffirm that boundary. Life affords so many opportunities, challenges and temptations to make decisions that are contrary to what we hold to be true for us. These variances end up as a split between our personality (ego) and our spiritual nature (soul.) The healthier we become the more integrated these two aspects of ourselves will be. I will merely mention here that once we have refined our skills in setting boundaries and have learned how to assertively reinforce those boundaries and are well on our way to becoming both autonomous and self-actualizing, there will be times when we will go beyond assertiveness into higher and more cosmic responses.

Once I took my car in to be fixed and found the garage mechanic grouchy and nasty. In my mind I went through all the possible assertive responses I could have used, but instead, I merely looked him in the eye and told him I knew his job was a difficult one and that I just wanted him to know how much I appreciated the care and good service he always gave to my car. Later when I went back to pick up the car, he greeted me with a smile, walked me to my car and explained he had washed it twice because it had rained after he washed it the first time. He opened my car door while telling me about the playhouse he was building for his children. That day we forged a camaraderie that remained the entire time I needed his service. It was also the day I learned it could be appropriate to go beyond assertiveness.

And often, life is full of paradoxes. When faced with challenges that are emotionally painful, we do need to grieve, but we also need to give ourselves spaces from grief. Any given event, no matter how traumatic or intrusive, is not the totality of our being. It may be all consuming and feel like it's all we are in the present moment, but other aspects of self still exist and need room for expression as well.

If we are doing our inner work properly, it most often requires outer *Action* as well. A friend writes: "During a very painful experience in my life, the emotional hurt was so intense and the shock and loss so overwhelming that it threatened to consume me. It was at that point that I began to pray for guidance, willing to do *anything* not to ever have to hurt that much again. As is usual with prayer and soul growth, the answers began to emerge and I knew precisely what I had to do. I had to take charge of my own life, be responsible for my own happiness and stop relying on someone else to make me happy. I knew that from the cosmic viewing place, all was in divine order and, ultimately, this experience was for my highest good. I realized some of the early emotional issues surrounding my fear of abandonment needed to be worked with, and I knew one of my values was to learn to love unconditionally and learn to release and forgive. I truly believe that we choose (either consciously or unconsciously) to be hurt or not to be hurt. But while I worked with this information and my understanding of all three quadrants, I was deeply aware that some immediate outer physical changes needed to happen. This is where I knew that I needed to take *Action*. I faced the situation as squarely as I could at that point and realized the first necessary step was to remove myself physically, and because it was my most viable and realistic choice, geographically from the situation. I decided to make a contract with myself that allowed me time to experience my grief process and neither repress nor deny my loss, but at the same time, I put a limit on it. Each time

I allowed myself to experience the pain and cry, I would set a timer and say to myself: 'Sweetie, cry as loudly and as deeply as you wish, but in thirty minutes (or two hours) when the timer goes off, you will get up, wash your face, put on fresh clothes and go somewhere or do something (and I'd specify exactly where or what) that allows you a new perspective.' I realized that even under those painful circumstances, I still *needed* to make room to enjoy a coastal sunset and to laugh at and enjoy a child's antics as she played in the sand. I *needed* to send a "love note" to someone who was being extremely supportive. I *needed* to stay in touch with the fact that while that person had been in the center of my existence, they had not been *all* of my existence. While sadness may have been the uppermost emotion, I still needed to make space to allow other facets of me to shine through, and the more I did this, the more healing and integration begin to move in and through me as well. One thing I've learned about myself, and I find that I'm not alone or too different than most people, is that I'm good at grief and victimhood. I can get going, gain momentum and throw a six month pity party (or if I really put my heart into it, the rest of my natural life time pity party!) However, the key word here is "*if.*" In re-parenting my inner child, I find it's as necessary to set limits on her as it is to set limits on the child in our outer world. My inner child needs to be heard and allowed to express her deepest feelings, and she needs unconditional love, but she should never be left totally in charge of things. She needs the loving guidance and limits set by my adult self, and she needs to be taught the cosmic perspective of my God Self. Left alone to her own devices, she is not only loving and spontaneously joyful, she can also be rude and incorrigible.

"So after removing myself physically from the painful environment I found myself occupying, and setting certain limits to keep healthy grief processes and unproductive victimhood separate, I decided to look at what other behaviors or adjustments I needed to make in order to reclaim my life and create my own happiness. As long as I continued to hand others the responsibility for my happiness, I also gave them my power, and I became a puppet on their string. At this point, I realized that I needed to be involved in some productive activities that capitalized on my strengths and interests and that I could feel good about doing. Therefore, I set about looking for places and activities that I might like to explore. I joined a Women's Healing Circle at a local YWCA. I joined a local Writer's League. I committed myself to daily self-growth activities. In short, I began to take positive steps toward creating a life that did not revolve around having any one person, place or thing in my life. Once again, I created a life of independence and diversity, which is certainly the healthiest lifestyle anyway, for it leaves one free to follow one's inner guidance and creativity. It gave me *space and freedom to follow Spirit!*

"I often made and wrote out contracts with myself, particularly in the beginning, for it's not easy sometimes to discipline oneself. I would offer to pick someone up and give them a ride to wherever I was going, thus, making it more difficult to back out without a good reason. With these steps, I returned to a more balanced, healthy, and happy life."

Changing our behavior is often called for if we want to lead a healthy existence and make life work for us. An alcoholic, or an addict of any kind, must modify their life if they are to shake themselves free of addiction. First, they may need to make time to join a twelve step program, they will probably need to stay, for a time, away from functions where alcohol is served. They will certainly need to refrain from keeping alcoholic beverages on hand, at least in the foreseeable future, and they will need to find other meaningful things to do that do not include their drug of choice. In short, they will be making many drastic lifestyle changes and modifying many of their former behaviors and habits in order to pursue a new and healthier lifestyle.

Most challenges in our life call for some modifications in our behavior. Only when we are willing to change some of our behaviors, do we solidify the inner healing processes and become able to function at higher levels. Individuals who are recently divorced or widowed find themselves needing to drastically rearrange their lives, and they usually find it necessary to engage in new activities, new support systems and new ways of moving through daily routines. If they fail to do so, life can become dull and meaningless and they end up feeling depressed and without hope for any kind of meaningful future. While these changes in behavior need to be in tandem with the other three quadrants and are not always sufficient unto themselves, they are still one of the necessary steps that lead to wholeness.

During the summer of 1969, I spent time in Los Angeles with Dr. William Glasser and his staff studying the concept of *Schools Without Failure* as outlined in the book of the same title. There were, of course, many benefits gained from that experience, but understanding the importance of using contracts as a viable force in teaching children responsibility was one of the most beneficial. I have used contracts with myself, with my own children, with students and with other adults. Each person writes and agrees to the contract and to specific responsibilities contained within it, as well as the direct consequences that will result if the contract is broken. If dealing with children, the adult helps to set up both the behavior and the consequence. Learning to write contracts that are concise and reasonable and that result in appropriate behavioral changes, becomes part of the process. Often the child or adult will see they were unrealistic or over-confident about what they could reasonably succeed in doing, or they see that the consequences were either too harsh, too mild or detrimental to obtaining the desired result. When that occurs, we sit down together again and examine the flaws of the previous agreement and rewrite the contract in more realistic terms. This becomes a skill that is acquired over time and brings tremendous insight and opportunities for growth in and of itself.

When I make contracts with myself, I have often shared them with someone who will help hold me responsible. For the most part, that is no longer necessary, for if I feel strongly enough about the need to modify something in my life, I also have the will to do it. However, if I doubted for a minute that I might not keep a contract with myself, I would have no qualms in soliciting help from one of my trusted friends. They love me enough to hold me accountable.

The contract is a written agreement to accomplish a specific goal, often within a specific time frame, and often contains the self-imposed consequences if one fails to keep the contract. With children, the adult is responsible for holding them to it and for imposing the consequences. Remember a contract with oneself demands just as much integrity as one made with another person. If one chooses not to do a written contract, often the natural consequences will be more than sufficient to impose its own penalty. The technique of using natural consequences as a way to teach children to make responsible decisions by suffering the logical and natural consequences of their bad decisions is well defined in the books on: *Parenting with Love and Logic* by Foster Cline and James Fey.

In the midst of all this talk about taking responsibility and action to create what we want and need in our lives, I must throw in still another paradox. It is possible in certain situations, the strongest action we can take is to *do nothing* and *wait patiently*. If we are obsessed with doing *something* even if it's wrong, then we will need to pull back and learn to wait. It is a positive action step to withdraw and do nothing if we need to stop being co-dependent and "fixing" things for others. When we stand back and allow others to take responsibility for working out their own problems, it may feel as though we are doing nothing. And, indeed, "nothing" is the most responsible course of action for us to take in that moment, but it might require a real modification of our previous impulsive behavior that is prone to rush in to rescue.

It has been said that luck is really a combination of effort and attitude. When we look around and think that others are just plain lucky, we fail to look at extenuating circumstances surrounding their so-called luck. Most people are helping to make their own luck. They just don't sit back with hands outstretched for the divine giveaway, instead, they see the synchronicity of events in their lives and they act on those events. In other words, those who seem to have all the luck, also, are often the ones willing to take the necessary action to bring their good into fruition. They generally have a healthy attitude about themselves and work to establish confidence in their own capabilities and possess a positive outlook.

Steps for Taking Responsible Action

The following process might be helpful in understanding how to determine both your choices and the actions you may ultimately take, as well as to distinguish between your desires vs. need. Perhaps you need a different car; here is one way to process that need.

What do I want?

A luxury car

What do I need?

Reliable transportation

What will I have to do to own a luxury car?

Work two or three jobs

What will I have to do to fill my needs?

Put in a few hours of overtime

Options:

Be willing to give up my life for a car

OR:

Look for a good used car or buy a new compact car.

Action

Since I need reliable transportation and do not have the cash or cash resources, I will begin taking on five hours of overtime each week or pick up a part time job, using the extra cash to make a car payment. I will restrict my spending (specify the area) in order to make a monthly car payment. I will be looking for a car in good condition, but I will not spend more than is absolutely essential at this point in time.

Many challenges, physical or emotional, can be resolved in a manner similar to the above. Practice this exercise when working with this quadrant and see how helpful it can be in aiding you to face both the reality of the challenge and to assume the responsibility for taking appropriate action in order to meet your own needs and get your life back on course. Evaluate, plan, act powerfully!

Summary

This quadrant deals with the ways in which we will often need to take ACTION in our lives in order to live up to the basic system of values we espouse. When we look at our behaviors in light of what we regard as our values and face the reality of our lives, it becomes evident that some changes will need to take place. We often need to modify our behavioral patterns, set boundaries around what is appropriate and not appropriate, and then learn to communicate those values and boundaries. Others cannot honor our commitment if we don't express it clearly.

ACTION STEPS

➢ Look over the list of values that you wrote down in response to the questions in the quadrant on *VALUES*. You may need to modify or change a behavior in order to live more in line with each particular value. Write it under the value listed.

➢ As you look at the area/s that you need to change in order to live up to your stated values and goals, what are the appropriate boundaries that you are going to need to set? On yourself? On others? Take as long as you need to respond thoughtfully and write down the boundaries that you will need.

➤ Begin to experiment with effective ways to communicate these boundaries to others. You may want to read one of the books on Assertiveness Training.

➤ Record all your responses in the notebook you started in the section on *VALUES*. Take plenty of time to do this exercise and revise and update it from time to time as your skill and powers of observation sharpen. *Remember: Practice Makes Perfect.* (Or at least it makes for progress and improvement.)

CHAPTER FOUR

Synthesis and Inner Healing

All too frequently, we find the "adult self" is no longer
In charge, and our behavior harkens back
To earlier times and places.
The "inner child" has just taken charge and we are
Reacting to ancient memories.
-Ione Jenson

Have you ever found yourself behaving in a manner that was totally opposite from how you would have liked to behave? Have you found yourself yelling or being abrupt with someone when you knew they had done nothing to deserve such anger, and yet, you felt helpless to stop the tirade? Have you found yourself retreating from a situation that called for assertiveness because you were afraid to stand up for your own best interests? Have you found that often your life is lived around fear, guilt or shame, and that "shoulds" dictate how you spend a great deal of your life energy? Do you find that you consistently place the demands, needs or wants of everyone else, no matter how frivolous or shallow, ahead of your own? When you do take care of yourself, do you feel guilty for having said "no" to someone else's request? These are just a few of the questions that will help us begin to see our need for inner exploration. The truth is that we dont have a fixed identity. We express many facets or sub-personalities that are all part of us. There is the adult, but also the inner child. There is both the brave one and the fearful one, and the list goes on.

No one comes through life unscathed. Everyone has some inevitable wounds that occur in the course of living, and since "earth school" is just that, a place for learning lessons, we all have ample opportunities to experience many "ups and downs." Huge numbers of people still live unconscious lives and believe that if everyone else was perfect, their own lives would be perfect as well. Of course that is untrue because we all create, consciously or unconsciously through our thoughts and actions, a large portion of our lives.

Once we become aware or *conscious* of our participation in the construction of our lives, things can gradually, and sometimes even dramatically, begin to change. We are not, nor have we ever been, solely victims of circumstances; we have merely been unconscious of our own evolutionary journeys.

Psychology used to believe that babies were born a blank slate, and religion taught in terms of predestination. However, a more accurate picture shows that from the beginning we contain those central spheres of energy that are pure spirit, the genetic DNA of evolutionary influences over billions of years, personal DNA which is the genetics and history of our family of origin, our particular soul's purpose, and the patterning of our particular culture. These factors all come into play as our personality and ego takes shape in the external world and under the influence of those who live and care for us in our early years of dependence, as well as those who will influence us as we continue growing throughout our lifetime.

As we become more and more consciously aware of our participation in the *co-creation* of our lives and of our world, we also realize change must first occur at the level of individual consciousness and permeate upward into all our religious, political and social organizations and cultural structures. If enough individuals consciously and sincerely evolve, I believe that one day they will rise up and lead the countries of the world in a more conscious and humane manner. With that kind of enlightened leadership, everything will change. We are beginning to see some glimpses of this arising around the world, and while it is true there are still only glimpses, and often fleeting ones at that, none-the-less, they are happening. The Age of Conscious Evolution, globally, is showing up in its early stages even now.

So much of our life is lived as a reaction to outer circumstances. When we find that we are *reacting* to events instead of *responding* from a thoughtful state of mind, we can be certain that some archetypal energy or negative programming in our past has taken over and it would behoove us to do some exploration and healing. We are not talking about being egocentric and selfish; we are talking about valuing ourselves enough to understand our own motives and inner processes. When we become consciously aware of what is happening and why it is occurring, we become more effective in responding appropriately. It ends up benefitting not only us, but it also benefits those around us.

There's a real difference between excuses and reasons. Excuses are rationalizations that represent an unwillingness to change. They are designed to "get us off the hook" and we do not expect to, or see the need for, change, nor is there any intention to learn from what has transpired. Reasons, on the other hand, while helping to explain a certain behavior or reaction, still ask us to examine and, perhaps, begin to deal with and heal certain things from our past. They also may well call for us to change some things in our life. Reasons can aid us in our journey toward enlightenment, clarity and responsibility. Excuses are a way of saying, "I'm a poor victim, so understand me, give me latitude, but don't expect me to change or do anything about it!"

When we explore our reactions and understand the part of our past they emerge from, then we are able to begin to work constructively with their energy. The more we love and understand ourselves, the more we are able to love and understand the other people with whom we live and work. When we are able to see our childhood dramas and creatively work with and heal them, it naturally follows that we begin to see another's childhood dramas as well, and we can be helpful by responding more appropriately.

If we can see why someone has behaved as they have, we can better understand it, even though we are not willing to excuse it and we may ask for it to be changed. If someone yells at us in abusive language and we understand this comes from deep childhood wounds, we might be able to refrain from taking it too personally. However, even though we understand, we will want to take decisive and positive action. We may begin by asking the person why they are afraid, or if they wish to calm down and then come back and explore the issue for positive solutions. If we can do this in love, we might be able to be the catalyst for helping this person heal in some measure. If, however, this person is not willing to explore or learn, or if they continue the practice of verbal abuse, we will need to set some healthy boundaries and firm limits on our interactions and around what is or is not acceptable to us. Should that fail, we may choose not to share physical space with this person any longer. If we are healed enough to respond in this manner, we may be able to do so without fear or anger, without acting like the victim, or without accusations and finger pointing designed to make the other person feel shame. In addition, we can understand that all of this has been presented as an opportunity for us to learn, and it has been our lesson to learn not to tolerate abuse. The other person's lessons will be learned when they are ready, and we can contribute to their cumulative learning by valuing ourselves. All the various forms of relationships come to mirror for us either unhealed areas in our lives or to bring needed opportunities for us to learn and grow.

So by understanding the reasons behind both our own behavior and the behavior of those around us, we can begin to draw healthy boundaries. In doing so, we heal even more and the ripple effect begins to permeate many areas of our life. There are many ways inner healing can begin to take place, and we will attempt to explore several different approaches by which you may wish to facilitate your own process.

I can only touch on a few methods that I have found viable and very helpful in my own journey. There are a multitude of others, some of which I have tried or studied. Others I have only heard about. The Institute of Heart Math has many, many good processes, and one I have used effectively is the "Freeze Frame" technique. Visit their website for more information. I also use "The Healing Codes" and like the fact that they also deal with cellular memories and events not available to the conscious mind. A friend of mine also swears by a method called: "Tapping." I know that with the richness of the Internet all of these resources can be located and explored in-depth. Here are just a few of the ways that I have used successfully over the years and that have proven invaluable for helping me to enter into what we have come to term: Conscious Evolution.

The Child Within

Long before the current inner child movement gained momentum through people like John Bradshaw, Earnie Larsen, Melody Beattie, Charles Whitfield and any other number of teachers of the concept, I was introduced to the wounded child living within each of us back in the 1960's. At that time I was working with people like Agnes Sanford, (who wrote many books on the subject of both healing and inner healing) Aron Abrahamsen, Cliff Custer and Ruth Carter Stapleton, all of whom were leading workshops on the need for working with childhood wounds. In those early days, Agnes had termed it "healing of the memories," and later it came to be called, "inner healing" or "faith imagination." We were using tools such as guided meditations or directed daydreams to facilitate getting in touch with the painful memories in our life, thus allowing us to dialogue, listen to and love the child within. It was, for the most part back then, done in a more Christian context by bringing in Jesus or Mary the Mother to help with the healing and sometimes the re-parenting. Other archetypes were used when the person seeking healing was of another faith. It was, and still is, an extremely effective technique, and the use of positive archetypes can still play an important role in the healing process. I feel I had such a head start by realizing very early just how important inner dialogue is and understanding the energy we call the inner child.

Even though there was a growing awareness about the inner child during the last decades of the twentieth century, the vast majority of our population still lack insight regarding the impact those energies can wield over daily life and interactions. Watching the political scene at all levels of government, the daily interactions in every workplace and in every family, one will observe a multitude of instances in which the "adult" personalities are no longer in charge and the energies of the inner children have taken control.

In the workplace, which is where we spend a very large portion of our waking hours, we are most likely to encounter the inner child both in ourselves and in our co-workers almost endlessly, and more often than not, in very small and seemingly inconsequential events. People often react to things as they did when they were children, and when these natural tendencies and behavior patterns begin showing up, being able to both understand them and work with them creates a more healthy environment for all concerned both at work and at home. When we remain stuck in these emotional charges, nothing changes and we sacrifice freedom for victimization.

Even our personal finances are often controlled by how our early families viewed money. Did they overspend? Were they thrifty? Were you raised during the depression or during a time of affluence? I know two sisters raised during the depression, and while their outer actions are very different, both are responding to the same early experiences in their family of origin. One saves relentlessly because tomorrow there may not be any, and her sister spends everything she has because her philosophy is to "eat, drink and be merry, for tomorrow there may be none." Those inner child energies keep the first woman from enjoying many of the amenities life offers, and the same energies keep the second woman from ever attaining any financial security.

When we live from the unconscious level, we are in control of our lives far less than we realize. Whether you are being obstreperous or overly nice, psychologically speaking, you are reacting in the same way you did as a child. Have you thrown a temper tantrum lately? If so, your inner child may be in need of a "time out." Consciously we know our spouse or boss is not our parent and our co-workers are not our siblings, and yet, very often we react to them in the same manner we reacted to the members of our family when we were young. If we live unconsciously and do not become aware of and acquainted with the inner child, nothing will change, and we sacrifice our true freedom for the status of victim. It might even cost us our job, our relationship or our home and family. Once we understand just how the inner child affects our personality, we can capitalize on the strengths that energy also brings, and we can learn to put healthy boundaries around those aspects that behave inappropriately.

In working with people on their parenting skills, I find one of the best methods of helping them see and become committed to positive parenting techniques is to first have them return to their own childhood and begin thinking about the people who empowered or dis-empowered them as children. Next they list the qualities of each type of personality and think about why those qualities either empowered or dis-empowered them as children. From there it is just a small step to look at the ways they parent their own children and begin making comparisons. As they begin to use some of the inner healing techniques on their inner child, including a technique called "*Overs*" which enables them to go back in their minds and visualize things being done more appropriately, it not only aids in healing for themselves, but becomes an active model for dealing with their own children.

Since we are human, all parents make mistakes. Inner healing, in its healthiest form, is not the process of assigning blame for everything in our lives that is not right, but rather is an attempt to correct faulty information that we have carried with us from childhood or, perhaps from the past. Cellular memory is a valid concept. It's an attempt to learn about ourselves in order that we might use the information to create healthier, happier and more productive lives. Messages ingested from childhood carry such great power and impact, precisely because we are so young and vulnerable and feel so powerless to change things when they are impacting us and the adults in charge are not protective. In fact, those very same adults may be the ones responsible for inflicting the pain, or may be so impotent due to their own childhood pain that they are as helpless as the child they need to be protecting.

So in seeking healing through this four quadrant process, exploring the issues of the inner child as a part of this third quadrant will be one of your biggest commitments to inner healing. Without working with and understanding this vital energy, it will be hard to execute lasting change. All of the following processes for inner healing can aid you in your inner child work.

"May I Have Overs?"

An effective technique for learning new ways of handling challenges and daily events is one I began using in the early 1970's and labeled: "May I have overs?" Back then my sister Gin, who was thirteen years older than I and who was going through the stress of raising teenagers at the time, made a statement that started me thinking. She was laughingly recounting some of her son's latest escapades and ended by saying: "If I had overs, I don't think I'd have kids again, because I don't think I was cut out to be a mother!" It's more often referred to as "do overs," but I still prefer "May I have overs," because we are usually asking for permission from the person we have wronged.

As that phrase, "If I had overs," rolled around in my mind, a thought ocurred to me. I still had youngsters at home and was teaching young children in the public school system, and it seemed to me that on some things perhaps we could, indeed, have overs. In letting the phrase roll off my tongue as well as my mind, I instinctively knew that children would relate to the terminology, so an idea was born. It also became apparent to me that it was not only a concept that would be helpful to children, but one that was equally applicable to adults as well.

Most of us are reactive. When we are under pressure or sudden change or challenging events happen, we tend to react. Very often we look back and think: "Oh, if I could just have done this or said that," or "I wish I'd handled it differently." Out of this retrospective state of mind, comes the concept of "May I have overs." "Overs" are an opportunity to empower ourselves and others as well. This process can encourage us to find alternative ways of meeting everyday challenges. It is also a way to teach ourselves how to respond to issues rather than being at the mercy of our reactive instincts. It's a process that allows us to explore, to practice, and to come up with some new and more productive ways of responding.

Is there a person who can truthfully say they have never been guilty of reacting? We all react to some degree, out of our own "garbage" and our own unhealed shadows, and we can all profit by learning and practicing ways of *responding* rather than just *reacting*. This is not to say that spontaneity and positive reaction does not have its place, but reactive behavior is often unkind and potentially harmful to us and those people or things who are the recipients of our reactions. If life is a series of projections, if it is a mirror that reflects for us our shadow selves and gives us opportunities to learn and grow, then we need a system for utilizing the rich possibilities that it offers. The process called "Overs" can be that vehicle.

As a beginning teacher of young children, when too many children were even legitimately needing something from me and I was feeling overwhelmed, I would occasionally find myself being a little too short or impatient with a child. After having a moment to reflect on what had transpired, it was so good to be able to put my arm around the little one and say: "Johnny (or Suzy) I'm sorry, I just reacted to you because I'm feeling tired, and I'd really like to do it better, may I have overs?" When said sincerely, most children won't refuse. We would resume our places where the incident had occurred, and we would both play it again. This time I responded with more understanding, and as a result I also became more skilled in handling pressure and stress. I learned new ways of responding during those years of both working with and loving young children, and I will always be grateful to my "little" teachers.

As time went by, the children would sometimes ask me if I needed "overs" and were quick to point out when other children should do "overs" as well. Often, when either the class or an individual child's behavior needed correcting, I could quietly ask: "Do you need overs?" and they would usually agree. Eventually, a few children began to ask for "overs" for themselves. It was a process that gave us all a good opportunity to find better ways of responding to one another.

One of the distinct advantages in the actual playing out of alternative behaviors in a process like "May I have overs" is that it touches deep levels of our inner being. It can be helpful to say: "I'm sorry," or to verbalize possibe alternatives, but in the act of practicing the alternatives through role playing, another dimension is added. By adding the bodily involvement, the feeling tone, and the dialogue, both people are given the chance to "try on" and practice the new response, thus making it a more holistic experience. It also affords the chance for instant, "on -the-spot" exoneration, forgiveness and inner healing. *Overs* is a technique that keeps us "current" rather than leaving us with "unfinished business," and it has the potential to prevent someone from carrying a grudge, suffering a wounded spirit or carrying around a scar. It also allows the person who is given *overs* to move from feelings of guilt into an opportunity to learn and grow and to avoid making the same mistakes again.

If the other person should refuse to give you "overs," it may be that you need to allow them to vent some feelings about the hurt or pain that your behavior brought up. Given a safe place and manner in which to explore the emotions, another will usually come to resolution and be both ready and willing to give you "overs." This exploration is also good "grist for the mill" in helping the other person understand the ways they may hurt others as well. Even the adults with whom I lived and worked found it acceptable to ask for a chance to rectify their unacceptable behaviors, or to gently ask when feeling unfairly assaulted by another, "Do you need *overs*." Giving a person a chance to try doing something again, is much superior to jumping in and fighting back. Naturally it is best if you have agreements regarding this technique before asking, but I have used it occasionally without agreements or without the individual even knowing what I was talking about, and it has often been successful.

If in the heat of the moment "Overs" are not possible, remember there is no time frame for reaping the benefits of this process. Situations can be discussed and replayed even a week, a month, or a year later. After my sons became adults, occasionally when I remembered something about their childhood that I wish could be done "over," we talked about it. Not morbidly nor to dwell on the past, but as a way of allowing them to integrate and heal some of their inner child wounds. In working with wounded adults, I have become aware of how healing it would be for their "inner child" to hear its parents actually admit unskillful behavior (anger, child abuse, incest, abandonment, unfairness, etc.) and say the simple words: "I'm sorry." I want my adult children to know my humanity and vulnerability and to know, that while I did the best I could at the time, I am still open to learning and growing from *all* of my life's experiences, past as well as present.

What would happen if a family set aside an "If I had Overs" night? A night where each member of the family would take a few minutes to look at their week and decide what they would like to do over. It might be an incident at home, at work, or at school. The family could be supportive and helpful in looking at alternatives for each member of the group. It could be a time to affirm each person's ability to begin responding in a more positive manner when similar circumstances presented themselves in the future. Using "Overs" is an excellent way to learn alternative ways of responding; try three or four different ways of redoing any one situation and then decide which feels best and gives the most appropriate results.

It is always good to remember that the events and actions that occur in the outer world are reflections of our inner world, even when they sometimes appear exaggerated. When our youngest boy came to live with us, he mirrored so much of my disowned "baggage" that we needed lots of "Overs." Have you ever *felt* a child coming home when they were still a block away? Since this child so often came home from school in a foul mood, I would brace myself before he ever hit the back porch. I would practice, alone, how I would play it differently the next time he came in the house and sometimes I was successful and sometimes I was not.

I discovered that when he came home feeling grouchy over something that happened in school, if instead of reacting heatedly to his mood, I could acknowledge his bad day and ask if he'd like to talk about it, he often would. Even if he communicated begrudgingly at first and in an aggressive tone, he soon calmed down and was in a much better frame of mind. It was such a revelation to discover how my own reaction or response made a difference in our interactions. Over our years together we both learned to play our parts very differently, and as I learned to play my role more effectively, he learned to play his part better, too. As I looked at him and saw my mirror reflection staring back at me, so did he look at me and see his mirror reflection looking at him. By the time he was in high school, we could both readily admit that we were just alike. It even became funny and a point of understanding between us. When he became very ill in August of 2000, and during the weeks before he died at age 37, he and I could communicate honestly and effectively. He would call every evening or two and would talk for an hour or more, and even though he was, in many ways, closer to his dad and brother, I was the one he called and opened his heart to and discussed his fears, and deepest feelings. I attribute that deep inner connection we shared to our ability to grant one another *"Overs."* We had come to realize how many *positive* qualities we mirrored for each other and how much each of us had mellowed and grown over the years. Since those first harrowing days of our coming together, we both learned to be less reactive and more skillful in responding to one another. How true it is that the child we have the most trouble with, is the one most like us. The one who comes to reflect our own strengths and weaknesses and to teach and help us to grow and to evolve.

By "redoing" situations in various ways, we begin to discover how the tone of our voices, our hidden agendas (manipulations) help influence and often determine the final outcome of the interaction. This discovery can help to form values that will lead to integrity and honesty and to an interdependence which does not rely on manipulating or using others. Everyone needs to learn processes which empower them to develop win/win relationships with those people with whom they live, work and play.

Psycho-Synthesis through Dialogue

The use of dialogue is among the most revealing and healing of the many processes one can employ for self-understanding. I first became familiar with this technique through Gestalt Therapy. Fritz Perls, a German Psychiatrist, used the two chair dialogue technique in his work, thus giving us one of the most effective tools for healing and integrating the shadows and/or splits that occur in the human ego-personality. In fact, there was an article written sometime in the last decade of the Twentieth Century that the Medical World had endorsed the two chair dialogue technique as the most effective therapy available for the integration of sub-personalities in people suffering from *Multiple Personality Disorder*, now re-labeled, *Dissociative Identity Disorder*. Of course, it took well over three decades from the time Fritz was demonstrating the technique and multitudes of people were benefitting greatly from its use, for the Medical community to accept its effectiveness and to advocate employing it. At least some medical personnel are now seeing and using many of the more proven alternative healing techniques.

Dialogue may be used to talk to the inner child, it may be used to talk to the shadows or sub-personalities we meet in our dreams or that block us from achieving a better and more expanded life. At times, I find it necessary to dialogue with the part of me that procrastinates or that behaves in ways I don't care to act. Often it is the child within me, but it can be other aspects of myself that want expression as well. We also have push/pulls that speak from our adult needs and that ask to be recognized and honored. I have a hermit self that likes quiet times and wants to be alone, and I have a cosmopolitan self that likes to be social and involved. There are times when these two rational and valid adult energies need to sit down, present their needs and points of view and then make compromises and unbreakable agreements as to how and when each can have its need filled. These are the times when two polarized but very important aspects of me sit down together, and through dialogue, set up a win/win situation that pleases them both. They each have the ability to see one another's perspective and understand one another's need, and they are both willing to cooperate in finding a balance that works. However, there are times when I have needed to give them a formal "conference time" so that one energy in its enthusiasm doesn't take more than its share. They are very good about cooperating with one another now, but in earlier years they had some pretty heated arguments before they learned to honor one another and understand the importance that each played in my well-being.

We may dialogue by writing the dialogue out on paper. Some find that method too time consuming so they prefer to do it out loud. However you choose to do it, it's helpful to record the dialogue so you can listen again and pick up any innuendos you may have missed. Sometimes the tone of the voice, or the particular word chosen can have a great impact on the overall meaning. It's so easy to get caught up in the dialogue that we forget, at the conscious level, exactly what the exchange has been. The recording provides us with the opportunity to get fully involved with the dialogue, and yet, we can be the observer/listener when we go back over the recording. This makes it possible for us to become an objective counselor to ourselves as well. Some people find the very writing of the dialogue, which involves the kinesthetic sense, is more helpful to them. The slower process works best for their particular needs, so it is imperative that everyone find the way that reaps the most benefits and produces the best results in their life.

If you are interested in trying to dialogue, put out two chairs and proceed as follows. Designate one chair as the person or object that you are dialoguing with. It may be your inner child, or anyone of a number of sub-personalities such as: the fearful self, the procrastinator, the angry self, the hermit self, the part of yourself that sabotages, the inner parent, the judge or critic, the spiritual self, the counselor or advisor within, etc. Or that chair might represent an inanimate object that appeared in a dream. An example might be a rock in the road that you cannot get past to arrive at your destination. The second chair will probably be your conscious adult self, or in the case of two opposing personalities, perhaps one chair would be the antagonist, the other chair for the protagonist. In any case, a chair will be assigned to each personality taking part in the dialogue. Once you have decided who will participate in the dialogue, you are ready for the next step.

Now you are ready to decide which personality will begin the dialogue. It's often wise to start with the conscious adult self and begin by asking the occupant of the other chair just what it needs or what it would like to communicate to you. Then switch to the other chair. It often helps to describe yourself as you try to slip into that role. You might say for example: "I am the 'Hermit self', and I like to cozy up here in the woods of Northern Idaho and just read and write to my heart's content. I'm wearing jeans and a sweatshirt, my Birkenstock shoes and no make-up." This description helps us enter into that particular mentality and then we can proceed to answer the question by stating our needs. The Hermit self might say something like: "you've been so busy being social lately that I haven't had time to fill my needs. I need you to slow down and give me some time to do the things I need to be healthy. I *need* time to read and to think. I need time away from people to be alone and quiet. You talk too much when you're with people and pretty soon my head is swimming and I am all stressed out, even though you may be enjoying yourself. I'd like you to consider my needs and give me some time off from your busyness."

Now the conscious self will respond. It might say something like: "yes, I know I have a difficult time saying 'no' sometimes, and I do need to be aware of your needs." Then, move back into the other chair and allow the Hermit self to respond. That aspect of self might say: "I'm really happy that you are aware of me, and I thank you for being responsive to what I'm saying. It really helps if you cooperate with me, then I don't have to make you sick in order to get time off." Switching chairs again, the conscious self might reply: "Let's determine what is a fair amount of time for each activity, and I will try to maintain the schedule we agree on."

This is, of course, a very quick and simplified version of a dialogue. Many interactions between sub-personalities will not only be lengthy, but will often be argumentative. It is not unusual for there to be anger and often heated exchanges between the various aspects of ourselves before any resolution can be achieved. It is good to allow any and all feelings/ emotions to emerge before attempting to find a win/win solution, because until emotions are spent, the various aspects of ourselves are like two individuals trying to resolve a conflict; we must feel that both our pain and our anger have been heard. Then, and only then, can we become receptive to finding workable solutions and enter into genuine conflict resolution. If we have repressed some part of ourselves over extended periods of time, we may need to have many dialogues over weeks or months before workable solutions and integration can take place.

With some issues, an on-going dialogue from time to time may be necessary. We may always be in need of dialoguing with our inner child, and also, with the Hermit self, because it is easy for us to forget how much we need times of positive solitude. Many times, after enough practice with the two chair technique, this dialogue will take place inside the mind without the use of chairs. However, for tough issues or for aspects not worked with before, we may still find the verbal (out loud) conversation with a recording device extremely insightful and helpful. For extended information on this technique, I like to recommend Fritz Perls book: *In and Out the Garbage Pail* or Barry Steven's book: *Don't Push the River.*

One other note here; the two chair dialogue technique is perfect to use with someone troubling in our life. We may find when we take their point of view, we often gain clarity and understanding that we had not considered before. That alone might be enough to change our interactions with that person and handle matters differently. The Course in Miracles says: "I can choose to see things differently," and when we follow that advice, everything else changes as well. I once heard a quote from a famous theologian that stated we cannot judge another person, regardless of what they might have done, because that may be their last lesson before they reach perfection. I don't know if that statement is true. I don't know if it is not true, but what I DO know is that when I perceive people in that context, I am a more compassionate and better person!

Gestalt Clearing Technique

As with our previous discussion about communication and the exploration of emotions through the two chair dialogue technique, the process of *Clearing* allows us to find acceptable ways of expressing deeply felt emotions of anger or hurt. It seems the more ways we can find to clear ourselves of pent up rage and pain without injuring another person, the less likely it becomes that those emotions will be expressed later in deeds of violence or passive aggressive behavior.

Most of us have used the term *hate*, and dutiful parents and teachers have told us it is wrong to hate. However, if our anger is intense, it becomes the one word that seems strong enough to adequately convey the depth of our feeling. Therefore, perhaps "hate" is a reasonable word to use for emotional release and clearing, if we learn to use it less generally and more precisely, and if we differentiate between the act and the actor.

As in Assertiveness Training when we learn to stop saying, "you make me feel angry," or "you make me feel worthless," and we begin to take responsibility for our own feelings and responses, so we can also take responsibility in the act of clearing out some of our more deadly emotions. Assertiveness Training teaches us to say, "I was angry with you" or "I felt worthless after our encounter," thus owning our own responses to a particular situation.

The process of clearing allows us to do likewise, and it even permits us to use the word "hate," but it does not allow for generalizations. Sometimes a powerful feeling of release comes from being able to use the word "hate" as a valid response to an event. Thus, in the process of clearing, it is not allowable to say: "I hate you," because this is a generalization, and there is something likeable in everyone whether we want to admit it or not. However, it is valid to say: "I hated it when you said I looked like a hag last Tuesday at lunch." This statement is very specific, the word hate is directed at an action not an individual, and it allows for the depth of the anger/hurt to be fully communicated and cleared. Clearing can be an important tool because it can prevent the build-up of hostilities that could eventually get vented in subtle or in other unhealthy ways.

Healing Through Dream Work

One of the fastest and easiest ways to understand the shadows that dwell and lurk within each of us, is through dream work. Primitive cultures and ancient societies have all recognized the significance of dreams. So many of our attitudes, actions and reactions spring from the repressed and unconscious realms within and are hidden from our conscious mind. Dreams allow us to bring into our conscious awareness those parts of ourselves that we have tucked away into the deep recesses and have often disowned. They also bring to our attention our needs, our desires, our hidden talents and abilities that are yet untapped, and the solution to many of our waking dilemmas.

Dreams are among the greatest of messengers from the depth of our own soul and from that realm of unlimited intelligence that few of us tap into during our waking hours. Yet, they are among the most ignored of all gifts. Even the most casual of glances through both the Old Testament and New Testament of the Bible, shows that God or Divine Mind consistently revealed itself in dreams. From Genesis to Revelation, dreams were used for guidance; Joseph was constantly warned, in dreams, when and where he would take Jesus for safety during those early years of his life.

Truly, dreams have become God's forgotten language as our culture has sadly moved from the heart and intuitive level into the more sophisticated, scientific head level. For as important as thinking, logic and reason are, they can never be a replacement for the *Spirit of Truth* that comes from the very deepest levels, nor a substitute for that inner voice that has the capability of tapping into sources of information not obtainable by reason, thinking or logic. Jesus, one of our great avatars stated: "Let those who have eyes see, and ears hear." He was alluding to the fact that understanding also comes in ways beyond our five senses and must be understood by the heart.

Thanks to Carl Jung, modern day "seekers after truth" are once again brought to the realization that dreams come to bring important messages to the dreamer. In his book, *Man and His Symbols*, Dr. Jung shows the validity of the collective unconscious as well as that of the masculine and feminine principles (anima and animus) that reside within all humans. He shows evidence that strongly supports his thesis that a common language, as well as a personal language, is resident in each dreamer and that this common language, referred to as archetypes, runs through mythology, fairy tales and our own dreams. We literally live out many of these archetypal patterns in our daily lives. We often call this dream language, *Universal Symbolism.*

Men like John A. Sanford and Morton Kelsey, Episcopal priests by ordination, and who were both spiritually directed and Jungian trained, added much to our understanding of dreams in relationship to Spirit. And people like Ann Faraday, Patricia Garfield, Tony Crisp, Jack Downey, Fritz Perls, Stephen LaBerge, Erich Fromm and Louis Savery, among others, have also added rich dimensions making dream interpretation a many faceted experience.

DREAM RECALL

For those who say they don't dream or don't recall dreams, here are a few hints that may help in that process.

> ➤ Develop a personal interest. Recall is greatly aided by an active interest. Reading books about dreams, sharing your dreams with others, or attending dream workshops are excellent ways to stimulate the remembering of dreams.

➤ Write out your intent and the reasons you want to remember your dreams.

➤ Get to bed at a reasonable hour.

➤ Prime the Pump for dreaming by telling yourself that you will recall your dreams on waking.

➤ Have a recording instrument by your bed. Put pen and paper or a voice activated recording device within easy reach.

➤ Review a book on dreams or your dream journal before going to sleep; it is an excellent mental set for stimulating dreams and dream recall.

➤ When awakening, lie quietly in the same position you find yourself. Then gently try recalling the dream.

➤ If it is not possible to recall or to write down the dream in its entirety, write down the major symbols and elements. This will often be enough to help you recall it later.

➤ Start at the end of the dream and work backward. This often works like a charm.

➤ Share your dreams.

➤ Act on your dreams. Each positive response to dream information, sets the stage and opens the door to more dreams and to a more expansive dream life.

Here are just a few general ideas to help you begin interpreting your own dreams and a few examples that might help you see some of the many levels and purposes served in our nightly adventures.

Guidelines:

➤ Before moving on to the metaphorical interpretation, the dream needs to always be considered literally in the first instance and examined for signs of objective truth such as warnings or reminders.

➤ If the dream makes no sense when taken literally, then work it through as a symbolic statement of the dreamer's feelings at the time of the dream.

➤ Most dreams are triggered by something on our minds or in our hearts, so the primary objective must be to relate the dream theme to some event or preoccupation of the previous day or two.

➤ The "feeling tone" of the dream usually gives a clue as to what this particular life situation is all about. For example, if the feeling tone of the dream is miserable, then the dream was likely sparked by some miserable situation or feeling in the dreamer's life.

➤ Common dream themes are likely to indicate common areas of human feeling or experience, but within these broad limits, each theme can mean different things to different dreamers according to the individual's life circumstances at the time of the dream.

➤ The same dream themes may occur from time to time in the dreams of the same dreamer and have a different specific meaning each time according to the dreamer's life circumstances at the time of the dream.

➤ Recurring dreams or nightmares *are important---heed them*! Dreams do not come to tell us what we already know, unless it is something we know but have failed to act upon, in which case they will come again and again, often in the form of nightmares, until we do act upon them. So if a dream seems to be dealing with something we are quite aware of, we might look for some other or deeper level of meaning.

➤ A dream must resonate inside the dreamer. It needs to make sense to the dreamer and move them to change their life constructively. Dreams come to expand, not diminish us.

➤ If a dream *shocks* you, do not hide from it. Every human being has every feeling that anyone else has ever had, so do not feel alone. Everyone will, at times, dream of topics such as sex, nudity, homosexuality, lust and other such things our culture has taught us are repugnant. However, they are instead, just merely the signs of our humanity. They are often symbolic of other things as well. The act of intercourse in a dream may symbolize hidden or denied urges, but it may also indicate the desire for deep unity and oneness with another person. Poets and writers have always referred to such communion as "intercourse." If the dreamer recognizes the dream as a true physical desire but acting upon it is inappropriate, remember that such feelings are natural drives that may once have been necessary to our race survival, but that does not mean we need to act upon them now. The dream may have been a warning to avoid situations that hold potential problems. The thief and murderer potential dwells within us all, but so does the Buddha and the Christ, and we are all responsible for what we choose to express in our outer lives.

In the 1960's as I began my own journey inward via dreams, there was far less printed material available to guide me. However, I first learned a simple technique which aided me in gaining insight into the language of my soul. Since many dreams are from our personal psyche, this is the level we will concentrate on for helping you begin the interpretation your own dreams. I will, later on, discuss in more detail the various levels in the dream state. This method is by no means the only way to interpret dreams, for many techniques aid in interpretation, but as a basic place to begin, it is very effective, so we will discuss it here.

The first step is to record the dream as fully as you can remember it and write it down. A notebook works well for this. Remember to record the date of the dream. Here is an example from my own dream file:

"Melody was outside my house, barefooted, and I urged her to come in and meet my friends. I sat down on the left end of the couch; Melody came and, lying down on my right, stretched out and put her head in my lap. She was crying and saying she should abandon her lifestyle, her search for truth, because people rejected her for it.

I held her head in my arms and assured her she must not change her lifestyle, her search, for I needed her way of life in order to be who God had intended me to be. I assured her that I needed people like Melody to forge the way, and I begged her not to change anything. She agreed as I felt great waves of perfect love for her. I picked up a tissue and dried her eyes. It was a time of great depth and love between us."

Now that the dream has been recorded, go back and underline every noun in the dream and occasionally a significant verb, and once you have underlined them, list them separately on a sheet of paper. The next step is to start allowing your mind to do some word association and record every thought that pops into your head whether or not it seems reasonable or logical. Here you will see how I executed the process in the dream I just recorded:

➤ Melody.......a real person in my life, counter-culture, a real seeker, open-minded, considered by many in our community to be "on the fringe," loving, spiritually very attuned, ahead of her time.

➤ Outside......to be outside looking in, outside as opposed to being a part of the "in" group.

➤ Barefooted.......to be vulnerable, without protection from the elements, not socially acceptable, to be "bare," without being "undercover"

➤ Couch......a place of comfort, a place to relax and to lay down your burdens, living room

➤ Head.......intellect, thinking, logic, reasoning, guilt

➤ Lap.......place of comfort, submission, warmth

➤ Lifestyle.......the way one chooses to participate in life, a choice, a philosophy, declaration of who one is, what one values

➤ Truth.......the search for the meaning of life, what is our purpose for being on earth, seeking the *Ultimate Good*, God, Universal Laws

➤ Arms.......place of comfort, love, warmth, peace, acceptance, strength

- ➢ God.......Good, Truth, Love, Justice, Peace, Spirit, Cosmic Mind, Creator, Organic Process, Divine Intelligence
- ➢ Perfect Love.......God, Truth, Spirit
- ➢ Tissue.......absorbent, soft, drying, "they shall wipe away their tears"
- ➢ Tears.......release, emotion, deep feelings

Once you have completed the above, go back and see if there are any puns. Dream time has a wonderful sense of humor and frequently uses puns to get the point across. In this dream, one pun stands out: Melody. While she certainly represents a living, counter-culture person in my world who is *very comfortable* with her chosen lifestyle, she seems to also be a pun for finding that place of "harmony" within my own life circumstances.

The next step is to examine your life at the moment and search the events and feelings of the last few days for clues. I immediately saw the connection. At that time, I was the wife of a minister in a traditional church setting and in a community of only 500 people. I was under a great deal of inner push/pull trying to walk in two worlds. At times I felt it would be easier to "play the role" expected, and yet knew I could never retreat from my expanded spiritual journey. Just a few days earlier I had recorded the following in my daily journal:

"I have a growing awareness that my spiritual search is frightenting to some people, particulary in this community. I have had statements come back to me that people think I'm 'weird, far-out' etc. I also have wondered: 'Should I give up the whole journey in order to be socially acceptable or the common kind of Christian?"

As is evidenced by the conflicts of the present, I could easily see the relationship between the dream message, my word associations and what was happening in my life at the moment. Much of the time, there will be an obvious and direct connection.

Now, think back and get into the *feeling level* of the dream. If the dream has produced fear, anger, resentment, remember back and find a time in waking life when you have experienced those same feelings and examine the circumstances for a connection.

In this particular dream, just thinking about how Melody felt in the dream brought tears, frustration, and feelings of rejection. It was easy to see that Melody was a part of me, and the feeling it produced when I thought back to the dream was a sure clue that my dream was revealing my quandary.

Fortunately, as dreams so often do, it also showed me the direction I needed to take. It was evident that I knew I needed to have, and that I deeply loved, this "truth-seeking, counter-culture, fringe" part of myself. She was absolutely necessary for me to be who God had intended me to be. From this message of the night, I knew that I could not give up my search. I knew that I must embrace this part of my life; I must dry my tears and move forward in a Spirit of faith, love and truth. And so I have, from that day on, never again questioned what I was here to do, nor have I slowed my steps in my personal psycho-spiritual journey. It is the all-encompassing passion for everything I do.

Let me review the steps, and I strongly urge you to practice it on several dreams before moving on to the other methods presented.

> ➢ Write the dream on paper. (It is advisable to begin a dream journal that will make for easy reference later) Date the dream
> ➢ Record the feeling tone.
> ➢ Underline the key words in the dream---usually nouns.
> ➢ List the nouns
> ➢ Do a word association on each noun
> ➢ List any puns used in the dream.
> ➢ Find and write down the basic dream theme.
> ➢ List recent events and feelings.
> ➢ List what you felt was the feeling tone of the dream.
> ➢ List your symbols in a permanent dream glossary for, undoubtedly, these symbols will be used repeatedly in other dreams. This is your *personal* symbolism.

Dreams, as earlier stated, often make use of puns. In my dream you will see that although Melody was a real person in my life and had all the qualities listed, she was also a pun. There must be harmony in our life between the conscious and unconscious aspects of our being.

There is also the area of universal symbolism that was previously mentioned, as derived from myths, fairy tales, etc. This symbolism runs through dreams regardless of sex, cultural or social conditions. It can be portrayed by the example of a circle which symbolizes whole, complete, unending in any language. Carl Jung's book, *Man and His Symbols,* is the best source for understanding this concept. However, in the case of this dream, it did not rely on universal symbolism to convey its message.

Dialoging, which we spoke of earlier, is another tool for interpreting the dream and unlocking its deeper mysteries. In using the two chair approach, all parts of the dream are taken as parts of yourself. In this particular dream, I could have dialogued with the bare feet for example:

Ione: "What are you doing out there?"

Feet: "Feeling pretty cold and vulnerable for one thing."

Ione: "Well, for pity's sake, why don't you 'cover-up'?"

Feet: "Can't you see that might be false? I could look pretty and I could be warm and comfortable, but then you wouldn't know what I really look like."

Ione: "Well, isn't it better to be warm and comfortable than to show yourself for how you really look?"

Feet: "Not for me it wouldn't be. To be comfortable and respectable at the expense of being free and without restriction wouldn't be worth the sacrifice."

The dialogue could continue for some time, but this is the general idea. Again, this is enough to show me what the unconscious parts of myself are feeling. I could have dialogued with Melody just as effectively, but the word association exercise was plain enough not to make that necessary.

Sometimes, there will be a *Top Dog* in your dream. That is the part of you that often says: *"you should, you ought, and you must.* This is how you heap guilt on yourself, and it usually carries the voice of mother, father, teacher, preacher, policeman, judge, and other authority figures, in its attempts to make you conform to someone else's expectations and concepts of what is right for your life. These top dogs should be dealt with and not allowed to control your life. You cannot make mature, independent adult decisions unless you are free to decide on your own and not feel compelled to make your decisions solely on past programming. Dialogue with those symbols who appear as authority figures in your dreams and let them know that from now on, you will make the decisions based on your own thoughts and understandings.

If there seems to be something in your dreams that keeps you from action, such as a telephone that won't dial, a car that won't start, be sure to dialogue and find out why your efforts are unproductive and why you are *sabotaging* yourself.

When a dream seems to have no resolution, you can take it into *creative imagination.* In order to do this, relax and go back into the dream. Deliberately dial the phone, make it ring, see the person answer and resolve the issue. This gives a message to the unconscious that you are determined to resolve the problem.

When someone is chasing you in your dreams, take it into creative imagination. Turn and face the person pursuing you, confront them, dialogue with them and try to find out why. Let them know you will respect and try to understand their reasons, but that you will not allow them to control you through fear. Remember, you are dealing with parts of yourself, and you are the commander of your own life so stay in charge.

Drawing a dream is an enlightening experience even when you feel you are one of those people who just cannot draw. Take a large sheet of paper and some crayons or colored chalk and begin letting color and form express your dream. You may be pleasantly surprised how much feeling and meaning will begin to emerge as you slowly let the dream express itself on paper. In our dream workshops, more than one person has been drawing a dream they just could not understand and found that as the drawing continued they were getting insights they had not been able to uncover before.

There are many types of dreams, and most dreams seem to be out of our own psyche and personal life. These dreams tend to give us insight into the "shadows" or unknown sides of ourselves, or to those parts we are well-acquainted with but have shunned, denied or repressed. We can learn and grow from this vast, rich store of "inside" information.

There will be those dreams that don't seem to fit into the personal growth category. Sometimes these dreams give us clear information or direction about some issue in our life, and that insight seems to be their prime objective. I well remember being about ten years of age when my mother got new Venetian blinds throughout the house. Fascinated, I pulled the blind in my bedroom up and down until it appeared that I'd broken it. Scared and postponing punishment, I concealed the broken blind behind the drapes knowing mother would not find it until after I'd left for school the next morning. I fell asleep that night and dreamed how to fix the blind. I awakened the next morning, climbed up on the bed and fixed it. I believed in dreams from that moment forward.

Other dreams seem to touch on being a *Holy Encounter*, a numinous experience. These dreams may feel fearful, but they are often accompanied by elation and a feeling that one has touched the *Divine*.

There are those dreams that give us a *Cosmic View*, dreams that give us an understanding of things far more vast than we have ever known before, and there are the dreams that seem to bring direct communication from the other side. My youngest son died at age 37 in September of 2000. He appeared to me within an hour of his death, in a vision that was as vivid as life itself, and he simply said: "See, mom, I am fine. Now you and dad be okay, too," and then he was gone. However, he has returned in dreams on several occasions since that time, giving me some most interesting insights into death and life after death. Some of those insights have sent me searching and some have created paradigm shifts in my thinking. But most assuredly, all these dreams have buttressed my faith in the ongoing life of the soul.

While there are other types of dreams that speak of possible past lives and other topics, the last type we will touch on here are those dreams that give us information that we cannot fully understand until, perhaps one day months or years later, the events of a dream unfold and we know, beyond any doubt, that the dream message was related to what is currently happening. Many such instances have been recorded in dream research, but I have also recorded several such instances in my own dream journals of the past 40 plus years. One of the advantages of a dream notebook is that we can then verify what has transpired since our dream took place and begin to appreciate that our unconscious mind is not bound by the laws of time and space. Only then can we be certain that a dream, that seems to be predicting a future event that was not accessible to our five sensory perceptions or by the power of reason and deduction, has been an extra-sensory understanding of the world around us. These dreams are often termed prophetic. One dream from my personal journal that proved prophetic was:

> *"I dreamed that I was in a large, beautiful mansion with crystal chandeliers. It was definitely a place of beauty and great wealth. However, a huge storm was brewing outside, and I thought I could close the shutters and minimize the effects of the storm. I began going from window to window in an attempt to get the shutters all secure. Even though I was working as hard as I could, I became aware that the job was too huge, the storm too violent, so I sat down and sighed: 'there is nothing I can do; I will have to let the* **Watergates** *flood.'"*

I sensed at the time that this was more than a personal dream and was aware that something in the nature of turmoil was brewing around our country. It was also evident that intercessory prayer on my part could not prevent the storm from happening or keep the damage from occurring; I had to allow things to take their course. When, nine months later, the news of Watergate flooded the media networks, I fully understood my dream.

Recording Dreams

If one is to take dream information seriously, there has to be a systematic method of recording dreams. A loose leaf notebook works well, because pages can be added. Record each dream on a separate page with the date. In this way, you can write down meanings, feelings and symbols when you have time or as additional understanding unfolds. It is also good to keep a file box with 3x5" index cards for a cross reference index. For example: In a dream containing a fire, write the word fire on one of the cards and then enter the date of the dream. In this way, you can add the dates of all dreams containing the symbol of fire on the same card. Fill out a similar card for each symbol that seems to recur in your dreams or that seems to have significant meaning or emotional impact in a particular dream. This system offers easy access to any dream information and proves helpful in locating dreams that one may want to refer to at a later date. You may devise a system more practical for you, but if you want access to dream information, don't rely on memory.

Conclusion

There is so much to be said about dreams and so much we are still exploring and discovering, but perhaps this gives the beginning seeker some concrete ways to work with dreams. There are also many good books on the subject and some of those are listed in the recommended reading list at the back of this book. Just remember there at two worlds, the physical and non-physical, or spiritual, and dreams help us build a bridge between those worlds. The vision, while awake, and the dream, while sleeping, are expressions from many levels of reality, ranging from our personal psyche, from our deep unconscious, from the collective unconscious and from the Cosmic Mind.

By the time you are 66 years of age, you will have spent 22 years in sleep. To feel those years are nothing more than a preparation for living the other 44 years, is to deny yourself a rich source of learning. *Happy Dreams......*

Guided Meditations

I have used guided meditations with inner child work, with emotional and physical healing work, and for other purposes as well. When working with dreams, we often do a re-creation of the dream after a thorough investigation of the feeling tone and have ascertained all the information available from the dream. Re-creating a dream after dream work is completed does not interfere with what the dream has come to teach, but it does help with integration and healing and is a completion. It truly brings the dream full circle as I have explained in the section on dream work. Guided meditations in the waking state also have the capacity to lead us to information about ourselves.

A word of caution about guided meditations before giving you some concrete examples of meditations that can be used. Guided meditations can be excellent tools for psycho-spiritual growth and healing. However, we cannot always take them as total unabridged truth. Just as dreams are not always literal, so the material that arises during guided meditations is not always literal. These experiences can be wonderful symbols about the psyche's contents or about the perceptions we may have, but they are not always literal and taking them at face value without investigating the facts is definitely, in my opinion and experience, not using wisdom. In both dreams and meditations, levels of reality can be blurred, and while we might view it as our reality, in actuality it may be a blend of several realities simultaneously. An example of this would be if one dreams of, or during meditation recalls, having been raped but is unable to tie it to any remembered event this lifetime. Among many possibilities that exist: it may be that it happened in another lifetime, or that one feels raped in a symbolic form.

There may be a grain of truth in the experiences that arise from some of our guided meditations, total truth in others, or they may be completely symbolic or even from another lifetime, but from wherever they emerge, they can, nonetheless, be very helpful in psycho-synthesis. Information that is not directly remembered, can still be most useful. It may be true, but if it cannot be consciously remembered, treat it as symbolic and work with it just as if it had been retrieved from the dream state. As a symbol from the psyche and personal unconscious mind, we can dialogue with it, draw it, journal about it, recreate it, or use it in any other healing manner. In this way, it is our personal truth but does not try to rewrite or impinge on what was outer reality. It's wiser to err on the side of conservative evaluation, for our objective is healing and it can effectively be utilized for that.

In this four quadrant process, we learn that even the most inept or outwardly evil among us, play a great cosmic role. Our work is to see ourselves in the larger scheme of things as well as in our smaller more personal arena. As important as it is to heal this small personal self, it can only effectively be done when we ultimately recognize and understand our small part in the evolving planetary soul as well. Both processes are very important, equal and absolutely necessary.

So with this one caution, here is a sample of a guided meditation that you may use alone or with a friend. In fact, if you are not used to doing inner work alone, it would be advisable to have a friend sit with you or to do it in a group. A lot of inner work can be done on one's own if we are experienced and not in need of professional help, but it is always good to have the feedback of others as well.

Treasure Chest Meditation

Sit quietly and take a few slow deep breaths. Now picture yourself in a meadow. Slowly allow yourself to feel the gentle breeze, smell the fresh clean air and see the vivid colors of the spring flowers. Below you lies a lovely little lake and there is a path that leads to it. You begin to follow the path, and when you arrive you are suddenly aware that the lake has very special qualities so you take off your shoes and begin to slowly walk into the water. Its warmth is so pleasant and as you walk deeper and deeper, you feel it flowing around your waist, your neck and then your face. Behold, the lake allows you to breathe easily under the water, so you venture even deeper. You walk around the bottom of the lake noting all the underwater life until you see something a short distance from you and go over to look at it more closely. To your amazement, you find it is a treasure chest and you try to open it. As you lift the lid, the contents of the chest are revealed to you. Take time to notice what is in the chest, its size, its shape and color. Now, gently replace the lid and pick the chest up and take it with you out of the water. Once you are again on the shore you see a person sitting on a large rock near the lake. You see that it is a Spiritual Being. (Here use any image that speaks to you: Jesus, Angel, Buddha, Guide, etc.) Walk over and hand the chest to this Being. Ask them to bless the contents, or ask to have them transformed if you do not like or comprehend the nature of the treasure. Talk with this Spiritual Being about what you found in the chest, about the Divine Plan for your life, or about any problem or issue that is confronting you. Listen to what is being shown or said to you. When you are ready to leave, you may leave the chest in the care of the Spiritual Being or take it with you, whatever feels right for you. Now make your way up the path and back to the meadow and then into the room in which you are now sitting. Either write down the experience, or if done in a group setting, discuss and share your experience.

Self Observation

One of the first necessities for inner healing is to hone the skill of self-observation. Without learning to be skilled in self-observation, it is difficult to move toward emotional wholeness. It is imperative for us to begin to observe and discover new facets.of ourselves. This is not a technique designed to judge or to be harsh on ourselves. In fact, the more lovingly we can do it, the faster emotional healing can transpire. If we can just take note of what we do, quietly take responsibility for our action (excludes blaming someone else for what goes wrong in our life) and refrain from harshly judging ourselves, then we have taken the first step toward finding healing and wholeness in our life. It often helps to gently laugh at ourselves as we observe our own unskillful behavior and remind ourselves that we were doing the best we could at that moment. However, we will know that as we become more skilled in developing an inner objective observer, we will also become increasingly skilled at responding and doing things better at the moment they are happening. The work here is to learn to love ourselves enough to honestly see our areas of ineptness without rancor or self-hate, and to acknowledge that we want to learn ways of living our lives more effectively. Our goal is peace of mind and good healthy ways of meeting the challenges of life in the most constructive manner. Nothing helps as much as gentle, loving self-observation and both the humor and *will* to move into a new mode of existence as we continually observe.

We will find that as we observe certain behaviors in ourselves, we will also note they emerge either from a place of fear or love. If we are responding warmly and well, we are feeling love and its accompanying emotions of generosity, compassion, empathy, and other positive feelings. If, on the other hand, our inner observer notices that we have not handled an event well, we can usually check out our "gut" and find that we are coming from a place of fear or one of its accompanying emotions such as anger, sorrow, pain, insecurity, etc. Should this occur, we can be certain that a lack of self-esteem or a lack of good boundaries is involved and some inner exploration of past experiences (inner child) and some inner dialogue is in order. We also find that once this is done and we have a bit of a handle on what has gone awry, we can then use one of the healing techniques we've acquired and work with the energy/s that need help.

It is here that I want to extol the virtues of a process I have used in recent years, and one that has come after having used many other processes, quite successfully, for more than thirty years.

"The Work" of Byron Katie

"The Work," as Katie calls it, is unbelievably simple, BUT, it isn't easy. One must be ready and willing to confront oneself with candor and uncompromising honesty. I am not certain if I was secure enough in earlier times for it to have worked so instantly and so effectively as I have found it to be at this point in my life. However, I am certain that for those who want to learn a relatively fast release from old thought patterns and ways of behaving, it is a way of cutting through to the core. "The Work," even used tentatively or sporadically, in my opinion, would bring immense benefits and help move one beyond fears and irrational beliefs to such a degree that one would soon be secure and comfortable enough to use it more often as the changes, challenges and transitions occur. Even as much as we would prefer to avoid discomfort, we need to be grateful for the events and people that come to give us opportunities to see ourselves honestly and to cleanse and break through the thought patterns that keep us from achieving a state of continual inner peace. Barbara Marx Hubbard calls these kinds of changes, challenges and transitions "evolutionary drivers" which force us to move forward.

After reading Byron Katie's book: *Loving What Is,* I went to her website (thework.org) and ran off copies of the worksheet which consists of four simple questions and a "turn around." I worked through these sheets in quick order to cut through the last vestiges of some long lasting threads of anger and pain. I was amazed at the almost instantaneous results. Then I found myself pulling out a worksheet each time something old or new rose up in my thoughts. It was incredible the ease with which clarity came and thoughts and old emotions dissolved. After some intensive experience with actually doing "the work," I found myself, and still do, less able to allow thoughts to disrupt my inner peace. When one appears, I instantly ask the first question: "Is this true?" I often dissolve in laughter at this point at the absolute absurdity of the thought or ego which would want me to buy into its lie and disrupt my inner peace. On those occasions when I do allow my inner peace to be shaken, I do a complete worksheet and very rapidly my equilibrium is restored and I again see so clearly how it all begins and ends inside of me. For the most part, the moment I observe a critical thought or judgment occurring, I go into "automatic pilot" and the four questions and turnaround come into play....that is if I even get beyond the first question before bursting into clarity and usually laughter.

In my personal journal I have an entry dated on May 1, 2003 that I would like to share with you.

> *"I love doing 'the work' of Byron Katie because it helps me perfect my humanity. It brings me closer to "doing and being" what I want to do and to being whom I want to be. It is the roadmap which takes me from where I find myself to where I want to go, and it leads me along my evolutionary journey into a more consciously evolved human being and into my role as a new 'universal human.'*
>
> *"I find it is not events or other people who put me under stress, thus disrupting my serenity and peace; it is my inner approach or attitude that puts me in a state of stress. Being ever self-observant and vigilant, helps me 'de-stress' from even the most challenging event or circumstance! 'The Work' is my vehicle for doing that quickly, efficiently, and effectively."*

Doing "The Work" does not negate the benefits of journaling, meditating, praying, working with my dreams, or employing other techniques as well. Often these disciplines bring up material that becomes *grist for the mill*. So, I take any negative aspects that arise or linger during those processes and put them through "The Work." However, Byron Katie's insights and her simple four questions and turn around process are hard to over-emphasis for those ready to confront themselves with the truth!

Visualization

Visualization is seeing, imaging, imagining an object, person, scene or activity. We are constantly in the process of visualization.

Some people think that they do not or cannot visualize. However, we visualize in different ways. Not everyone sees vivid clear pictures as on a movie screen. Some merely have an impression, others just imagine seeing something, or even just think about something. Most of us are unaware that we are always visualizing in some way and thus are in a constant process of programming our lives. Our expectations of what we think will happen, or hope will happen, or fear will happen, set a scene in our mind. Actually, we rehearse for most activities in our life. We can move forward in the direction we truly desire by becoming aware of how we are rehearsing and then by visualizing and imagining our desires as already fulfilled.

Many people get ready for any challenge in life (an earth school test) by fearing the problems and obstacles and seeing themselves tripping over them. This is rehearsing for what we don't want. Rehearsing for what we do want is visualizing (seeing and expecting) the positive desired outcome.

For example, Joe, a student who sees himself as a poor student is fearful before every test and sees himself confused and anxious. Jim, on the other hand, sees himself as a good student and a confident test taker who can come through. They both study for the same number of hours. It is not difficult to predict which one is likely to score higher on the test. Joe and Jim may not think of themselves as visualizers, but they are. We all are. Visualization is not a "far out" esoteric activity. It is a process we engage in every day, either consciously or unconsciously.

Dynamic Changes Through
Conscious Visualizations

> ➤ Better health
> ➤ The ability to channel healing to yourself and others
> ➤ Improved self-esteem
> ➤ Increased ability to love and be loved
> ➤ Clear up the past, forgive and be forgiven

> ➤ Finding more meaning and purpose in life
> ➤ Peace and harmony

The activity of focused, conscious visualization will help you change your life in the way you want it to change.

How Visualization Works

Imagination, the power of picturing, has been called: "the scissors of the mind." These scissors cut, shape, and create our reality and our life. We need to understand that the conscious mind is only the tip of the iceberg. The unconscious mind regulates body functions, remembers how to walk and do all those things we don't need to consciously think about. It stores memories; think how confused life would be if all memories had to be conscious all the time! The unconscious mind does an incredible amount of work for us. It is capable of doing much more if we give it the proper instructions.

How do we go about giving the unconscious mind effective and proper instructions? Our thoughts and feelings are the key. The pictures we hold in our conscious mind and the feelings we hold along with them are instructions to the unconscious mind to accept these pictures and feelings as our reality. The unconscious mind automatically continues with that picture of reality unless we re-program it.

If you want to become more self-assured and confident, picture and feel yourself being confident in a specific situation. Notice what it is like to feel confident. Say to yourself: "I am a confident person." At those times when you begin to feel shaky or unsure, bring your mind back to that specific confident situation and tell yourself again: "I am a confident person." In your mind, keep replacing what you don't want (insecurity) with what you do want (confidence.) You don't need to constantly think about picturing confidence. The conscious mind is free to be involved in its usual activities. The unconscious mind works to carry out the assignment you give it whether you are awake or asleep or engaged in other activities. You will gradually become more confident and confidence will eventually become an integral part of your personality.

Someone once said: "We are what we think about all day long." The unconscious mind takes everything we focus upon and stores it for us; it does not discriminate between what is positive and what is negative. If we channel negative unproductive pictures, thoughts, and feelings into it, it shapes negative unproductive outcomes. We know that our bodies respond to a fearful picture in our mind as if it were reality, creating specific bodily reactions such as sweating palms, shaking knees, knotted stomach, even if it is actually perfectly safe. Our inner pictures do have a definite effect upon us.

The good news is that we can change these negative inner pictures. The unconscious can be re-programmed for new and positive results. We can actually reshape our life experience once we know about and use the power of visualization.

Dr. O. Carl Simonton gained a national reputation many years ago for combining visualization with regular treatment for cancer. He would get to know his patients and then help them find a picture that was meaningful to them. Simonton feels that it is important for the individual to be able to feel enthusiastic and to really believe the scenario in the mind. The more the patient could do this, the more likely the cure. The technique of visualization is being used successfully in treatment all these years later.

Studies have been done revealing that teachers who were told that students with low I.Q. 's had I.Q. s higher than they actually had, treated them differently. As the teachers treated the students "as if" they were bright, the students saw themselves differently and actually performed better than anyone would have predicted.

The sports world has become more and more aware of the power of visualization. An experiment was done with basketball players where half of them practiced making baskets and the other half sat on the sidelines and visualized themselves making baskets. In competition, the visualizers performed as well as the players who had actually practiced.

Elements of Effective Visualization

> ➤ Add feeling to the pictures. Believe in the new outcome you are creating. Get enthusiastic.

> ➤ Add positive self-talk affirmations. Positive statements we make to ourselves help us feel and picture the desired outcome. The statements need to be phrased in the present tense with the focus upon what we want such as: "During my job interview I am relaxed and communicating clearly. I am poised and confident."

> ➤ Do your part. Suppose you're visualizing for a promotion and raise at work. Don't stop there. Look for ways to improve your job performance. Visualize yourself doing a better job and your boss appreciating it. Give your best, then expect just compensation. Give your best to the world and the world will give the best back to you. Giving is a prerequisite to receiving. Do your part.

> ➤ Face your fears. Sometimes we really want something and visualize for it, but it doesn't happen. Why? Because we may have actually programmed it not to happen with our fear that it would not. However, our fears cannot keep our good from us if we face them. With a pad and pencil write down all alternatives. And don't forget to take the cosmic view that perhaps something greater is being planned for you.

Visualization to Ease Fear

Every day see your fear in the shape of a black ball. See a beam of light begin to pierce it until it dissipates. Rejoice within yourself that your fear is leaving. As you get into it, you may find that your unconscious mind will help you by bringing to your memory the reasons for your fear and even some ideas for healing the cause of the fear. Our minds are wondrous storehouses of help and information. All we need do is set the process in motion.

Practice Visualization to Gain Confidence

➢ Draw a circle in your mind. Draw a square in your mind. Draw a triangle in your mind. You're visualizing.

➢ Picture a shoe. Is it a man's or a woman's? High or low? What color? You're visualizing.

➢ Look intently at an object, any single object. Now close your eyes and see it. If you don't see it the first time, repeat the process until you do. Now, open your eyes. Look at the object and notice a detail that you did not see the first time. Now once again close your eyes and see the object with the new detail. Repeat as often as you need to. Continue this process until you can close your eyes and see several details.

➢ Remember one of your favorite places. Close your eyes and reconstruct as much as possible. Describe it to yourself. Make this a continuing exercise. Every time you visit a favorite place, notice as much as possible and re-create it in your mind later. When you are feeling stressed, return to this place for a few moments.

➢ Practice incorporating other senses as well as sight into your visualizations.

  • FEEL: a gentle breeze on a warm summer day, hot sand beneath your feet and then the coolness as you reach the water's edge, or feel the softness of satin or velvet.

  • SMELL: fresh homemade bread, sheets that have hung outside and dried in fresh air, bacon frying, coffee perking.

  • TASTE: your favorite food, a lemon (does your mouth pucker?), a freshly picked sun ripened tomato.

  • HEAR: a waterfall, your favorite musical instrument playing your favorite song, a choir singing "Silent Night," the voice of one you love.

➢ When you first wake up, visualize or sense a warm golden light surrounding you, protecting you, and being with you throughout the day. Before you fall asleep at night, see this same light surrounding and protecting you throughout the night.

Conclusion

You can begin today to use this most precious resource, the power of your mind. This creative power is God-given. However, until we understand it and use it, we cannot reap the wonderful benefits of this treasure. The Bible tells us: "It is the Father's good pleasure to give you the Kingdom," and, "The Kingdom of Heaven is within." We have the power right here and right now, through the power of our mind, to transform ourselves and to become all that we can be. In truth, we are beautiful, capable, loving and loveable children of God. Let us begin now to fully claim our spiritual birthright.

Journaling

Journaling is yet another way we can use for self-observation and the many components that make up our life. Writing daily pages is a wonderful way to unblock our creative flow and to open our heart, mind and spirit to the life giving energies that often lie latent within. Frequent, if not daily, journaling is a way to emotional release, and there is some impressive scientific research that shows by the actual act of writing down your deep feelings and thoughts you can improve your physical wellbeing. One of these studies by immunologist, Dr. Ronald Glaser who has studied the effects of writing, was able to show in blood tests that people who wrote about traumatic experiences actually boosted their immune systems and the benefits lasted up to six weeks. While the physical benefits are awesome in themselves, they pale in comparison to both the emotional and spiritual benefits derived from the act of keeping a journal.

My spiritual journey would have been considerably slower and much less exciting without my attempts at journaling. That daily record of feelings, intuition, events and attitudes served as a release and as a balance. I could give vent to feelings that my personal nature, at that point, would not have allowed in any other form of expression. After these things were on paper and my mood had mellowed, it then became a matter of reviewing the events, the feelings, and evaluating my own "hang-ups," reactions or actions, to determine a constructive course of action in the event that life should offer me a repeat performance.

Sometimes, in a warm reflective mood, nostalgia would spread itself across the pages, one memory leading into another. Often, I would be amazed at how I'd really felt about an event in the dim, distant past. It is an excellent way to get in touch with things that lie back there, dimly remembered or completely forgotten, that still have some influence over feelings and reactions experienced in the present. The "Inner Child" still lives and feels with deep emotions, no matter how far we have removed that child from our conscious minds.

I well remember the afternoon, journal in hand, when my mind and heart found me back in Iowa in front of my childhood home. I was six or seven years of age that day. The weather must have been mild for I don't remember a coat or winter wraps of any kind. There was an ambulance in front of our house and two men had just put a stretcher, on which my father was lying, in the back end. Mother was climbing in beside him, and I was saying: "How long will you be there, Daddy?" He grinned, in an attempt to be light-hearted, and replied: Until they kick me out."

I recalled that my father had been having a great deal of trouble with a foot, which many months later resulted in an amputated leg, and he had been in much pain. He had paced the floor all night. And now the ambulance had come to take him to the Veterans Hospital some sixty miles away. This event occurred in the early 1940's; World War II had begun, so the best doctors and drugs were there. In those days, sixty miles was a two-hour drive on narrow, winding, unimproved roads, and to my child's mind, they might as well have taken him to Mars. As those moments were relived, I knew the child had really been asking: "Are you going to die, Daddy? Will I ever see you again?" There is no remembrance of any specific feelings then, except that I was a little scared, but as I recorded the memory in my journal some 35 years later, deep sobs and a rush of uncontrollable tears began. I mentally picked up that little girl and assured her that it was all going to be fine and that she would be cared for and loved.

The day that I relived those moments and quieted the child's fears, I also in some beautiful mystical way, felt a deep inner release from old fears and wounds. When looking back upon the experience of writing that memory, it is easy to see that the child's mind had not even been mature enough to comprehend what she was feeling, but it had been recorded in the depth of the unconscious and that event definitely needed to be confronted again. The healing and release that is experienced is hard to describe, but once you have experienced it, you know something deep inside has taken place.

At other times, joyous moments are recorded with happiness and enthusiasm. When deep feelings of love and oneness can be expressed in no other way, I take pen in hand and let it flow. It was in this mood that the following was recorded

Love Divine, All Love Excelling
August 15, 1974

"I cannot stop its coming or its going.
As an artist whose canvas catches the overflowing of the beauty his eye and spirit beholds,
Or as a poet pours his inner feelings on paper,
So must I release the overflowing love that pours through me and give it to those for whom its feelings overwhelm me.
It is beyond conscious control.
I can keep it from expression, but I cannot keep it from rising within my soul.
Nor can I bid it come.
My mind can make me empathic, it can make me sympathetic, and it can make me act in a compassionate manner,
But, it cannot make that full tide of overflowing Love come at will.
Love, whose only release is in the beauty of full expression
Perfect, unselfish, divine love that comes only from the Creator of all love. God is Love made manifest!"

Or on another occasion, it had been a long, hard day at school. I was working in Eugene, in a school of almost six hundred students. The days were long and hard, but it was an opportunity to work with a woman principal who was dedicated and who offered me many challenges for growth. At the end of this very difficult day, I stopped by her office to offer some encouragement when I caught a glimpse of a tear. There was nothing to do but to hug her, and the sharing of that moment was deeply moving. It is recorded in my journal in the following words:

Friendship

"A tear wends its way slowly and quietly
Down your face.
My cheek blends with yours in a momentary
Embrace,
And your hand reaches upward to rest
On my face,
We share the moment's pain, frustration
And caring love."

Another example I will share from my personal journal is an experience of profound meaning in my spiritual journey. My husband, Ace, was about to be ordained as a minister and I had never felt so "dry" in all my life. I wasn't at all certain that I could even go with him into the ministry. It was a crossroads in my life, and the future was very uncertain. I could not enter into a church community and pretend to believe something I did not. Something had to happen; for within me was pain and conflict and God either had to become REAL or I had to forget about Him altogether. No more spiritual fence straddling!

In the midst of all this turmoil, one of Ace's professors at Northwest Christian College was in a serious auto accident that claimed the life of his wife and critically injured him. I had never seen anyone go through such a crisis, such a long, painful recuperation with such faith and joy. George was an inspiration of faith and hope. We watched him make a magnificent recovery, and return to life, undaunted.

A short time after George's recovery, I had really hit a spiritual low and went to church one Sunday evening for what I hoped would be some answers. The answers came, not from the minister as would be expected, but from glancing across the room and seeing George. Memories of his courage and faith renewed me that evening in a quiet and powerful way. My heart and mind overflowing, I rushed home, grabbed my journal and put it down that I might always gain faith and courage from that experience. Many times after that writing, I reread those words and gained the strength to continue my deeply profound and meaningful spiritual walk.

To George

"I looked into your eyes
And heard your voice singing:
'I know, I know that Jesus liveth
And on this earth, one day will stand.

From your tragedy, and still
Bound by injury to a wheelchair,
You gave me the message of Easter,
You gave me the image of Christ.

Your unending smile in the face of sorrow,
Your will to regain a fruitful life,
Your Spiritual convictions in living,
All helped me know our God more intimately.

And then, one year later, we stood together
In the same sanctuary and almost the same pew,

And once again your dear presence
Answered my questions and made Christ live again!

The tears fell unendingly that night,
Your love surrounded me by your mere presence.
Life once again regained its depth of meaning,
And God used your strength to help me rebuild mine."

The journal can play an active part in integrating and in changing our lives, but remains an open-ended tool which neither restricts nor imposes limits upon our development. There are no rules and structures which say it must be thus. We are free to develop a method which best allows for our individual psychological and spiritual growth patterns. In that light, what is set forth on these pages becomes guidelines and suggestions for your own journey. With time you will find ways to meet your own needs and enrich your own life in your own unique journaling fashion.

One final and powerful way that journaling can be used, and which is my very favorite, is to seek the Divine Wisdom that seems to always be so readily available if we but cultivate the habit of listening. I now have many notebooks full of inspiration that has come to me over the years and often use my own journals for my daily devotionals. Below is an example of that process:

Question: "Who are you that so quietly and gently reminds me of a better way? Who are you, the ever present "watcher" and "objective observer" who reminds me to be patient when ego is short on patience, who reminds me to honor the earth by picking up trash I have not strewn on the lawn rather than seethe about my upstairs neighbors? Who are you who reminds me that I am one with all creation, equal to, but neither superior nor inferior to, everyone around me, and who reminds me that all things and all people are a part of one huge system, one life and one creation?"

Answer: "Whatever arises, pause and listen for my voice before you act or react. I AM that aspect of you that operates beyond time and space and with wisdom beyond your ego's ability to comprehend. Think peace, love and hope. Go to your heart space for there is your Divine Center, and there is where I, your God-self dwells. Your heart is your connection to ALL that is, will be or ever has been. You ask who I am, I am your true self, the expanded you who is not confined to time and space but who is part of the Divine Mind, the expanded, all knowing force of creation. I am not ego mind, but I am Spirit Mind or Christ Consciousness. You allow me a voice by listening to me. Listen carefully and live life in response to my voice, and you will always be blessed."

Here are some general guidelines which the beginner should at least consider:

➢ Use a notebook that can be permanently kept and easily added to, or subtracted from, as you desire.

➢ You may want to get a trusted person to agree that upon your death, those pages will be destroyed unread, unless for some reason you want it kept. If you are really honest and set forth everything you think and feel, it might cause some hard feelings or create misunderstandings among those people who did not understand your purpose. To mentally edit everything you write to please the eyes of a future reader, diminishes the value of the journal.

➢ Date the entries in your journal.

➢ Record dreams as a part of the journal, especially if you're using your dreams as a vehicle to the inner self.

➢ Be completely honest, do not "edit" or smooth over the happening. Write exactly what you see and feel at the moment. Constructive, real and lasting changes can only take place in the context of utter honesty.

➢ Go back in "history" and begin your journal from the earliest point you can remember and reflect on and record those past events. It is well worth weeks, months, or years of time to have a section labeled "Past History" and add to it continually for as long as you can recall those past experiences. They will often give you clues and insights into present feelings and attitudes thereby helping you see why certain things "push buttons" for you in the present.

➢ Remember the journal is not just a record of events, but an exploration of your feelings and relationship to those events. A mere recording of events is, in fact, a diary. A journal has much more than that to offer, for its meaning lies in the feedback it offers you for evaluating where you are today and for determining life changes that bring integration and wholeness to you.

➢ Use the journal to record meditations. When you have centered yourself in God and received a flow of images, words or insights, do record this wisdom that has come from the "Kingdom within." It is a vital part of your life flow and can bring with it rare insights and divine objectivity. Do not lose this inner wisdom, for it will produce opportunities for affirmative action. Some people meditate strictly for the silence so this would not apply, of course, to that type of meditation. However, many people around the world are also finding vast growth in using the type of meditation where one pays attention to the visual images, even if used only part of the time. (For a longer discourse on this issue, see Morton Kelsey's book: *The Other Side of Silence.*)

➢ Find a quiet time and space where you will be uninterrupted and can flow with whatever comes to mind and beckons for your attention. Daily journaling is best, but one should aim for three entries a week as a minimum. However, if nothing else, do it as often as you can, for even the most limited amount of time will bring some benefits.

➢ As we learned how to do earlier, use Creative Imagination to bring healing to events, past or present, that still hurt and cause pain. As I did with my Inner Child whose Daddy was being taken to the hospital, we can do much to heal our own psyches through this useful tool of "creative imaging." As we employ this tool, a Divine force beyond ourselves that is not limited by our time-space concepts, seems to become powerfully operative and releases a deep healing energy beyond our limited abilities to comprehend.

> ➢ Try as often as possible to take a spiritual or contemplative day, weekend, or week, where you can go alone, (or with a friend who shares the common bond in a search for truth) either fasting, or eating lightly and spending the entire time with the inner processes. Carefully record the experience in its fullness. In this way, no doorbells, telephones, or routines (such as meal preparation) interfere. It is truly a "time apart" and much good can result. For young adults with children, it might necessitate trading babysitting once or twice a month. But a way can be found, if one is serious enough about the journey.

> ➢ Record experiences and feelings as they are happening, if at all possible. Otherwise, record them as immediately as you can while the fullness of the moment is still at hand. Later as you reread and see the experience more objectively, then record the objective feelings of the moment, as well. Both feelings are valid.

A journal can make us vividly aware of talents or resources within ourselves that we may not have known we possessed. It can aid us in developing an awareness of our true identity.

As one looks back over the entries and over the weeks, months and years, it is evident that patterns and meanings emerge, and we can begin to ask: "What was the lesson in all of this? Did I learn what it came to teach me?" There is an inescapable inner continuity, a kind of thread that runs through the sequences of actions and reactions in our life and we see, at last, that events in themselves are relatively unimportant. Importance ultimately lies in our relationship to those events and to the lessons we have learned. Through journaling, we will find that we are so much more than our conscious mind. Thoughts and great truths are sometimes revealed, and we may find ourselves in awe when we read what appears on the written page and wonder just how we "knew" that. Do enjoy the journey!

The Presence Process

Michael Brown wrote a book a few years ago which was called: *The Present Process,* and even though it was published in 2005, it did not fall into my hands until 2010. At that point, two friends and I agreed to embark on his ten week program as it was written out in the book. We found it gave us a great deal of insight and helped us make some changes in our lives. We met each Wednesday afternoon for three hours to discuss the program, what our results had been during the week and to pose any questions or points we wished to explore with the others. Each week we were given a Presence Activating Statement to use for the following seven days. We used a connected breathing technique which Michael explained in the book.

At the end of the first ten weeks, one of those friends and I agreed to do it for a second ten week period; so three weeks later we started it for the second time. Both times we agreed that the component of the process that was central to the changes we felt was the activating statement which was directed at both our conscious and unconscious mind. That statement, frequently repeated each day throughout the week and combined with the connected breathing exercise that we did each morning and evening, brought up many memories and feelings to experience, to feel and to release as we breathed. I repeated the ten weeks alone later. While both of those friends, much younger than I, made their transitions quite suddenly and unexpectedly in a less than a year after we completed the process, I cannot help but believe that the Presence Process helped ease their final journeys and that their souls still carry the benefits.

Affirmations

Affirmations have a definite place in our healing and growth process. While it is not inconceivable that some people may have an instantaneous transformation, it is not a common occurrence and may only be in one area of their life. Most often growth is a process and, like an onion, we peel away layer after layer until we are able to heal and grow past issues and experiences that have occurred over our lifetime or that are lodged deep within our cellular memory. It takes strength and courage to view ourselves honestly and then embrace those parts that are not so loveable.

Feelings of frustration, anger, and other negative emotions arise from deep within, and when they do, we may feel guilty and helpless. Often, because we either don't know how to deal with them or we are afraid to admit to ourselves that they exist, we push them down and pretend they are not there or we project them out onto others and judge them harshly. Fortunately, there are ways to transform those feelings, but not without action on our part.

Affirmations are one way to begin the transformation process. Our unconscious mind acts much like a recording device, it records indiscriminately what we "feed" into it. If we feed our minds negative emotions and feelings, then our life will produce negativity. However, if we "feed" our minds positive, healthful and power-filled thoughts and statements, our outer life will reflect those same qualities.

Before beginning affirmations, whenever possible, it is best to find a comfortable chair and get your body relaxed. You may even want to image a white light hovering above your head and slowly penetrating through the top of your skull. As the white light enters, it cleanses and relaxes you. It continues to flow through your head and moves down into your neck, your shoulders, and down into your arms and hands, always cleansing and relaxing as it goes. Visualize or feel the light continuing through your chest, down your back, and through the abdomen, hips and pelvic region. From there it flows through your thighs, to your knees, down the calves of your legs and into your ankles and feet. You are now completely filled with light and are relaxed and ready to begin your affirmation/s. Keep your statements positive and say them with conviction and with as much feeling and meaning as you can while visualizing them as already manifested. As you feed this positive energy into your own conscious and unconscious mind, you are also setting the universal forces in motion.

The following affirmations are just some examples which you may use or which may help guide you in creating your own.

Affirmations for the Body

> My body is made of the non-aging, non-deteriorating substance of God. I revel in its increasing vigor, I revel in its perfect health. I revel that every cell, every atom, every organ of my body is filled with the divine life and love of the Creator, and is therefore perfect, even as God is perfect. I give praise for it, I give thanks for it, I bless it for being what it is, the outermost layer of my soul.

> Inhale, reminding yourself that the breath of life is the breath of God, and direct it to your eyes saying: "The breath of Life rests and restores my eyes."

> The light of life is the eye, and God is that light.

> God's pure life and substance are constantly renewing and rebuilding His Holy Temple, my body.

> I see myself as God sees me, perfect in mind and in body.

> The Holy Spirit quickens my mind and body and I am whole.

> The Spirit of God strengthens both my soul and my body and I rest in the peace of wholeness and health.

Affirmations for Peace and Relaxation

> God's mighty confidence and peace enfold me. The Omnipresent Spirit of God fills my mind and I am resting in perfect peace.

> I have faith in the Divine Spirit and I am protected. My life and affairs are all in Divine Order.

> I am harmonized, peaceful and poised in Spirit and in Truth and God's grace is sufficient for me.

Affirmations of Self

> ➢ I am a child of the Most High God, and since I am worthy of his creation, I am a worthy soul. I shall love myself, even as God loves me.
> ➢ I am willing to take the responsibility for all of my decisions, and I am also willing to take risks. I will give, take and love as my deep inner desires are led by Spirit. I am prepared to be fully and totally responsible for the outcomes.

Affirmations of Protection

> ➢ I now place a wall of living flame around me. Any negative thoughts, feelings or attitudes directed toward me will be transmuted by Divine Love and sent back to bless the sender.

Affirmations of Peace and Love

> ➢ I am at peace with all humankind and I truly and -unselfishly love all men and women. I now acknowledge the perfect law of justice and equality. I know that God is a respecter of all persons and every man, woman and child is my equal in the presence of God.
> ➢ I love my neighbor as myself, and I do unto others as I would have them do unto me.
> ➢ I am made in the image of Perfect Love and embrace all people as worthy of love.

Use affirmations daily or many times a day. The changes will begin to appear, and over time, you may be amazed at the changes you will feel within yourself. The more "programmed" you have been, the longer you may need to use a certain affirmation, but the changes will come.

No discussion of affirmations is complete without mentioning Louise Hay and the difference she has made with her teachings and use of affirmations. Her works are a rich source for affirmations of all kinds, and I urge readers to access the vast gift she has given to spiritual growth through her books, workshops and example.

Conclusion

There are many other noteworthy tools to help along the way. Not every tool I have mentioned will appeal to everyone, but I encourage you to give some of them a try and experience what works best for you. Since healing is our ultimate goal, it doesn't matter which approach you use, our Creator honors them all. It is our *"Intention"* that matters the most and ultimately creates us anew.

CHAPTER FIVE

A Cosmic and Evolutionary Perspective

All life and all events are just energy. They
Take the form and shape we give to them.
-Ione Jenson

The Cosmic Connection is both the beginning and the ending. It is truly the Alpha and the Omega, and as we start to work our way through the four quadrants to wholeness, it serves us well if we can always begin the process by affirming that whatever is happening has some order, meaning, and purpose. The goal is to use it for personal growth and for the good of the planet in so far as we are able. We need to be fully aware that even as the tides have their ebb and flow, so do our lives. It is certain that we will experience periods of intense joy, and it is equally certain that we will experience what is termed "the dark night of the soul." Both states contribute equally to the growth of the soul, and both conditions will yield to the power and energy of our thoughts and perceptions about them. When we learn to treat those two aspects just the same, we will have arrived at the place of non-duality.

It does not matter what path one follows, be it one of the various religions, an eclectic Spiritual journey utilizing truth from several, or the path of humanism. At the end of the day they all proclaim one basic truth, the importance of love and respect for others. It is from love that we look at the Cosmic Overview.

Reliance on Divine Order and faith in God, or trust in the evolutionary process, is not a passive pose. It becomes exceedingly active as we listen and act on the wisdom we are led to understand in those quiet moments of prayer or contemplation. Acting on the inner wisdom, as we are best able to understand it, is an important aspect of our Spiritual Life. Joan Borysenko in her insightful book: *A Woman's Book of Life: The Biology, Psychology, and Spirituality of the Feminine Life Cycle,* indicates there are behavioral models that link depression and helplessness. That seems reasonable to me, for when we think we have no control ovr the situations facing us, both helplessness and depression would be a likely consequence.

However, an unshakeable understanding and trust in Divine Order and in the Evolutionary or Organic Process which uses disorder and chaos, a breaking down or disordering of systems in order to reorganize and recreate higher forms and which incorporates the old as it rises to higher degrees of organization, is neither fatalistic or non-participatory. Rather it is the basic or core-value which gives one the stability, the wisdom, the love and understanding to interact decisively, compassionately, and often dispassionately, with the events and challenges that confront us individually and universally in varying degrees. It is the truth that sets us free.

Helping ourselves, others, and most certainly aiding our children to grow in confidence and with a sense of the importance of interacting positively with events while staying grounded in love and with the internal spirit rather than yielding to fear and helplessness, becomes a clarion call.

As in the quote at the beginning of this chapter where it is stated that all life and events are just energy, it behooves us to become more deeply aware of the power of energy that is projected through our thoughts. When we send a loving thought or prayer to another person, we are actually sending them energy which empowers them to a greater degree than they might otherwise have. Of course, in order to do this, we must keep our own thoughts and energy high, but in a strange, or not so strange, paradox, the more we send love and energy to others, the more that energy returns to and flows in us. Our alignment to The Divine as expressed in our daily lives and through our loving actions, as well as our inner times of connection during meditation, prayer and other spiritual practices, helps keep our energy high.

One of the major ways we dissipate our energy is through assuming the role of victim and by not taking personal responsibility for our lives and thus entering into co-dependent and enmeshed relationships. When this occurs, we are disconnected from our Source as we play out and re-enact the dramas of childhood. This, of course, is not productive for the persons involved.

A real exchange of energy that empowers both of the participants has neither attachment nor expectation. It thrives on the purity of intention. This type of energy exchange brings about incredible synergy and both individuals have the capacity to reach deeper and higher levels of intuition, insight, creativity, and wisdom.

Stuart Wilde, in his book: *"The Whispering Winds of Change,"* expresses his views on how our perceptions shape or alter our reality. And, indeed, he is right. How we perceive events and the condition we prescribe to any given situation then causes us to label them "good," or "bad" when the events themselves are neutral. Our interpretation has created our reality concerning that event. How often have we labeled something as "bad," and then, from a later vantage point we've been able to see that what we had labeled negatively was really ultimately good? It's been said that "life is a backward teacher, it often gives the test before we know what the lesson is about."

Even when there are evil actions and evil intentions, there are no evil souls and hearts. Only fear and love exist. We are an evolving humanity, and under it all, we are "gods in the making" and are a part of the co-creative forces in the Universal plan toward *Love*.

Several years ago a woman I met went through a traumatic, emotional divorce that she felt was the end of everything good in her life. However, a few years ago when we met again after not having

106

been in contact for a lengthy period of time, I noticed such a radiant, joyful glow about her. Her first words after our initial greeting were: "Ione, that separation had to occur for me to find myself and become all that I was intended to be. I had set myself up in such a co-dependent situation that I never could have attained all I was meant to do." She had finished college, had gone on to establish herself in an exciting profession and was anticipating even greater adventures. I couldn't help asking her if she could go back to the former situation and never have to experience the pain and trauma she went through, would she go. She gave me a resounding "no" and stated she had learned and grown so dramatically when pushed reluctantly into that "corner," that she now saw it as a pivotal point of significant value. She has never changed her opinion about it.

Had she been able, from the beginning, to see the larger picture or rise high enough above the situation to get a glimpse of the cosmic view, she may never have suffered to the extent that she did. Even if she had gone through an initial period of grief and releasing what had been, she would have had immense comfort from knowing what was awaiting her. In the words of a Unity minister friend of mine: "We only give up good for greater good.

The Course in Miracles teaches in one of the daily lessons: "I can choose to see this differently." Once we finally concede that there is more than one way to look at things, we can began to circumambulate situations and discover many different possibilities. Negative views are always possible, but then, there are just as many positive ways to view the situation as well. We need to ask ourselves: "Do I wish to choose to see this negatively and be miserable, or do I wish to choose to see this in a more positive way, trusting in ultimate good to emerge and find peace in the situation?" Remembering that the choice of how we look at things is always ours, we make our own reality and create our own happiness or despair.

Another close friend of mine went with me to a spiritual retreat one summer back in 1973. While we were there, we were given a 3" x 5" card and asked to write down the one greatest desire of our heart.

It would be kept in a prayer box and prayed over daily, and it would be returned to us in six months. When we received it, we were to open it and see how our prayer request had been affected. We both complied with the experiment, continued to enjoy our summer together and then returned to our daily work and life that fall. In November, I received a frantic call from my friend who was in tears. She had just been fired, after more than two decades as a successful, tenured high school English and History teacher. To say she was in distress, is a gross understatement. Suddenly, the light dawned on me, and I asked her if her prayer request earlier in the summer came into play in this situation. I could hear her gasp. She had been having some differences with the young new principal of the school and she had asked that those differences be resolved for once and for all. Of course, the resolution did not come in the way she had expected, however, it did arrive in the best way possible. She found a job in a business in the private sector. It equaled her former income, gave even greater benefits, and removed her from the drugs and gangs and unruliness of the public school scene where she had taught. She was much better off and continued with the company until her retirement many years later. Hindsight, they say, is better than foresight, but if we are willing to look for alternative perceptions and try to rise high enough above our current involvement with the crisis, we can usually get a glimpse of meaning and purpose in the events. Often, in the years before she made her transition, she told me how grateful she was for that experience.

This is not always an easy task and we will certainly be more successful sometimes than we will be at other times. But it is a process, and the more we practice, the more likely we are to succeed. If we can't rise high enough to see the whole picture, we can settle for affirming a faith in ultimate purpose and divine justice. When we have lived long enough and practiced looking for the *COSMIC OVERVIEW* sufficiently enough, we will come to know that time and distance will usually provide us with deeper insight and understanding. In retrospect, we can nearly always see clearly the deeper meaning and purpose behind most of the events in our lives and count that as a decided advantage in keeping stress to a minimum and keeping despair in perspective.

I worked and lived with other people in a spiritual healing community atmosphere for over 23 years. (For more information about the *Holo Community*, we have written about it in the book: *Women Alone: Creating a Joyous and Fulfilling Life*, Hay House 1995) One of our basic commitments was to psycho-spiritual growth for ourselves individually, collectively for our little community, and for all those who came seeking emotional support and integration or searching for a positive direction. When people would come feeling they were victims of poor parenting, I liked to ask them to close their eyes, to lovingly and consciously choose to dispense, for the moment, with their disbelief, and gently allow me to guide them back to a time before birth. We tried, from this vantage point, to see why their soul might have chosen the parents and the family situation they were born into. We attempted to visualize the archetype most comfortable to their spiritual perception or belief system (Higher Self, Jesus, Guardian Angels, Being of Light, etc.) standing there to help them understand just why they chose this particular situation. We attempted to look honestly at both the strengths and weaknesses of all involved and some of the agreements they may have made in the interest of soul development. Some amazing understandings can emerge from this exercise of faith.

In taking myself through this exercise many years ago, I discovered that the reason I chose a father who was sick a great deal of my life and who died when I was just 16 years of age, was so that I might experience the love of a wonderful father in my early years, but also that I might experience a mother with only a fourth grade education who had such a fierce streak of independence and pride that she found a way to maintain her family in spite of all the adverse circumstances that happened. This woman empowered me, by her very example, to know that women were strong, were capable and even under very stressful circumstances with very limited resources could create life in a positive direction. The fact that I had to work to help out and that I virtually had to pay my own way through college by various and sundry creative endeavors, only strengthened my understanding of how I could have almost anything I wanted if I was willing to make the effort to obtain it. When I started college in 1952, there were no student loans, grants, or many scholarships available. However, out of that came an understanding of my own will and determination and an appreciation for my education. Choosing a family without financial resources, enhanced my soul by forcing me to rely on myself and gain confidence in my own abilities. There were many other reasons I chose this family, and in spite of what may have appeared as weaknesses as well as strengths, each one contributed something of lasting value to who I have become. I must admit, I chose very well.

If we can begin viewing our family of origin as a family of soul choice, precisely for both its so-called strengths and weaknesses and as the perfect environment for the unfolding of our soul, we can begin to see the benefits of the particular family group we chose. We can see how their strengths taught and modeled the important lessons we came to learn, and we'll also see how their unhealed areas have often managed to strengthen us if we've capitalized on the opportunity.

In James Redfield's bestselling book, *The Celestine Prophecy*, the eighth insight shares how a child is the combination of the two parents and is to take elements from each parent and raise them to a higher level. I can certainly see where I did this with my parents. My father was an adventurer, my mother liked stability and roots. The two natures often came into conflict with one another. However, I have been able to combine my adventuresome nature with a sense of solid stability and create a wonderful life full of change and excitement within the context of responsibility and solid values. It is also interesting to note that our son has done likewise. Chuck has taken my intense interest in books and learning, my ability to communicate and understand feelings and he has put it together with his father's relaxed, unselfish, and uncomplicated lifestyle. In doing so, he is happy, intelligent, caring, and always probing for deeper meaning, but does so in a relaxed and easy going manner. Parents and families are probably not formed by accident nor by luck, but by soul choice and for the sole purpose of individual and planetary evolutionary advancement. If we are willing to view this larger perspective as a possibility, we might be surprised at the results.

What it eventually comes down to, is our willingness to expand our vision sufficiently enough to look for a larger meaning surrounding our seemingly small lives, and the willingness to peer into what might be the larger context of evolution and historical perspective. Once we have made the determination to see how our individual lives and sacrifices fit into the whole of humanity and into the total evolution of the planetary soul, things begin to make more sense. In short, the question seems to be: "How willing are we to take the events that happen to us and perceive them to be a small piece of the puzzle in what is happening to humankind as a whole? Are we truly a small part of a much larger whole? Does what happens to us, individually, influence or promote the good of the larger community even when it appears to be at our expense? Is it possible that our soul sometimes chooses, without our conscious awareness, to be part of something much greater than the finite life we are living, and in doing so, it thus ensures a larger movement toward the collective good?"

I am not certain how soldiers from any war, how people from concentration camps or those suffering from post-traumatic stress syndrome can ever hope to heal except within this larger context. It seems that unless we are willing to become a participant in viewing the possibilities of a larger picture as well as a participant in our personal growth, healing of inner emotional wounds is difficult, meaningless and, often, impossible.

Viktor Frankl, in his wonderful books entitled: *Man's Search for Meaning*, and *From Psychotherapy to Logotherapy*, shares how he found meaning even through his experiences as a Jewish political prisoner in Nazi concentration camps. He is a prime example and an extraordinary model of how the human spirit and the human will can work together to choose not only how it will perceive events, but how it will use those same circumstances to find meaning and purpose. He came to believe in what he termed the "last ultimate freedom." Liberty is external and that can be taken from us, however, freedom is internal and no one can ever rob us of the freedom to think and choose our internal response to outer events.

When all this begins to ring true, begins to call forth a response at deep inner levels, and when we feel in agreement with the premise that there is some measure of Divine synchronicity in our lives, we may wonder just how to go about finding that connection to the *COSMIC OVERVIEW.* We may begin asking what we can do to see and understand the deeper meaning behind all the events, welcomed and unwelcomed, that occur in our lives.

One way is to begin to understand the spiritual law of Cause and Effect and how our thoughts and actions create the outer manifestations occurring in our lives. Our Body, Mind and Spirit are all forms of energy, and our actions, our thoughts and our higher aspirations and intentions bring about the events we encounter. Our action, thoughts and intentions are like an echo and our life is a mirror which reflects for us the results.

Prayer

Prayer, since ancient times, has been a part of life for many people. Most major religions espouse rituals that include prayer and supplication. Some of these religions have formal ritualized prayers such as the rosary in Catholicism or the formal daily prayer times of Eastern religions. Still other religions subscribe to less formal methods, even down to the freewheeling conversational prayer practiced by some of the protestant denominations in Christianity. While prayer takes many forms, it is usually considered by most religions to be a major way of connecting with the deity being worshiped.

In the Bible, the disciples said to Jesus: "Lord, teach us to pray." When I was a child growing up in the church there was a hymn we used to sing about that scripture.

For centuries humankind has asked that simple, yet complex question, "how do I pray effectively?" It seems that at times our prayers are powerful tools, and at other times, we feel as though our prayers are a wasted effort. What makes the difference? What is the mystery behind effective prayer?

No one has all the answers, but a few brave spiritual explorers have found some keys that help. Larry Dossey M.D. who has written the book: *Prayer is Good Medicine* and who has done some controlled studies on the efficacy of prayer, found that people being prayed for fared better in healing than those who were not being prayed for. And an important fact emerged, it did not matter which religion or spiritual tradition was being used, they all worked equally well. Truly, "there is nothing new under the sun," only our re-discovery of that which has always been. In that light, here are just a few ways that prayer take place.

Prayers of Praise and Thanksgiving

This is perhaps the easiest of all prayers when everything is going well and the most difficult when things are going wrong. However, in some unexplained and yet mystical way, the prayer of Praise and Thanksgiving releases a power, an energy that is capable of changing the situation and, more important, our attitude toward the event. Since all life is moving energy and our thoughts actually create, or re-create our life, it would seem that we have shifted the "thought field" and the response is positive. A quantum scientist might have a better explanation.

Prayers of Forgiveness

Most religions teach some form of forgiveness, but none more vividly than the sentence from the Lord's Prayer: "Forgive us our debts, as we forgive out debtors." That line points to the fact that an ancient spiritual law of sowing and reaping is in effect here. We will be forgiven in the same measure that we have forgiven. I would hasten to add here that I am not speaking about God's lack of forgiveness for us, but actually about our own lack of forgiveness for ourselves. What we dislike or judge in another is a signal to go within and look for what we are judging in ourselves. The judgment of others often indicates judgment of oneself projected outward.

Guided Meditation/Visual Prayer

Over the years we have used guided meditations for this type of prayer. We do this visual form of prayer because it helps our unconscious mind to know how serious we are. The unconscious mind is like a child and pictures are better than words. The inner child needs a vivid concrete expression to feel forgiven. Here is an example of a meditation that could be used.

"Find a comfortable spot and relax. Close your eyes and find yourself in the Presence of someone who represents true spirituality to you. It might be an angel, Buddha, Jesus, Gandhi, or any other archetype that feels comfortable. When you are able to find that image, take a moment to really look and connect at the heart. Visualize them holding out their arms to you if they have not already done so. Move toward them and into the open arms. Talk with them about what you are feeling and ask for forgiveness for whatever is troubling you. Take plenty of time until you can feel the warm embrace of the arms around you and listen to the comforting words: "You are forgiven." "Allow yourself to stay in the embrace until you actually feel yourself melt into the other being and until you are truly One.""

Prayers of Release and Healing

Variations of guided meditations can be done when we want to release people or situations. We might do a meditation where we visualize ourselves giving the person or situation to the archetype of our choice and asking for a divine blessing on everyone and everything concerned. We may also choose to ask for greater understanding and to be made consciously aware of what our lesson might be and what is being reflected that we might learn and grow from the experience.

When we are seeking physical healing, the visual prayer in the form of a guided meditation can be very effective. Find a comfortable spot and surround yourself with light. And then taking that light, see it extend into your body and go to the area in need of healing. Hold that light in your mind, seeing it surround and penetrate the affected body part until it is filled and radiating with light and energy. Now begin to hold the image of a perfect body. Don't see the body as diseased, instead get a picture of the body part in its perfect state and hold that picture in your mind for five or ten minutes, two to four times a day. Do it for as long as necessary. It might take some time for change to occur, especially for the inexperienced person in this type of prayer, the power of deep concentration is not an easy discipline.

Intercessory Prayer

No discussion of prayer is complete without mentioning the power of intercessory prayer. It was alluded to earlier when I spoke of Larry Dossey's work. When I first discovered the potential power of intercessory prayer several decades ago through Agnes Sanford and her work, it was such relief to know that I no longer had to just feel helpless when someone was suffering either physical or emotional pain. When the person is physically present and open to the spiritual realm, we can often do a laying-on-of -hands or some type of "energy work" as this allows one to become a direct channel of powerful healing energy that comes straight from the Creative Field of all Possibilities. However, being physically present is certainly not a requirement or even an added benefit. Because we can transcend our concept of time and space, I have witnessed and participated in many distant healings. When praying for others in whatever capacity, we must be certain to be "pure of heart" and be perfectly clear about our intentions and prayers. We must not interfere in another's life or soul choices and prayer must never be a form of manipulation.

Prayers of Supplication

The prayers of supplication ask for favors from God, or in some cases from Saints. Whatever type of prayer is chosen, from the "please help me, God" to the more rote and memorized kinds of prayer, it can be used as a vehicle to help one connect to the Divine Source within and to that higher creative energy that flows in and through all things.

The degree of connection that we find with the Divine will be dependent upon our basic motives and intentions. If we are sincere about finding that inner quality of Spirit, the precise wording of the prayer itself is less important than the heart from which it emanates. Prayers are powerful, and we want to be certain that what we ask for is what we really want because we might get it. It behooves us not to take prayer too lightly, but at the same time, we must allow prayers to be heart "felt." The energy, the love, the desire for only the highest and best for both ourselves and others is necessary for effective connection with God. Prayer should never be a way of manipulating others to become, do, or be what we want.

Sincere prayers seeking for insight, wisdom, and Divine Order in one's life will result in increased understanding of the deeper meanings and purposes behind the events in our personal lives and in the larger world scene. We may never understand everything, nor may we ever see all there is to see behind every given challenge, but if we can get glimmers of the universal purpose that lies beyond the appearance, we will gain a perspective and a measure of peace otherwise not attainable. At the very least, we can embrace the Divine Mystery itself.

Meditation

Meditation was also explained in the Inner Healing quadrant, but it is also a process that brings us to a closer connection with the Universal or Divine Mind. Meditation has often been described as the other half of prayer. Prayer being that process of "talking to" God, and meditation being the process of "listening to" God. It is often referred to in some places as "listening prayer." The semantics that label the process are not important, least of all to the Divine, but the practice of meditation becomes a vehicle for making our connection with the higher life energies.

Barbara Marx Hubbard, in her book: *Birth 2012 and Beyond*, states that she writes out as clearly as she can, either her problem or what she wants to know. "Then I stop thinking and develop a poised mind and remain open to what is emerging. That means not going to sleep, and not going into profound meditation. It is deep listening. What seems to come through is higher mind, deeper intelligence, wisdom. Then I write without editing myself, without allowing my mental mind to interrupt the process. Often I find that the higher mind is much wiser than my mental mind."

Meditation can be a quiet time for introspection, a time for clearing the mind of the daily onslaught of words that clutter and confuse our thinking. If we will make time to sit in utter silence long enough, even twenty minutes is sufficient, we can begin to reach something deep and immense inside of us; we can touch something so vital that it helps us begin to put things in some semblance of order and to gain some kind of perspective and the power to confront the real issues.

If we are truly committed to finding our cosmic connection in order to understand the larger purpose behind our own small lives, we need to stop allowing our days to be so filled with daily routines and projects that gain momentum and take over our existence. Eastern religions have always honored the place of quiet and peacefulness within their spiritual practices; Western religions have tended to place more emphasis on and have honored the outer displays, or "works" as it is often called. We need both, and as Westerners, finding those quiet times consistently will prove very beneficial to our peace of mind and to our spiritual understanding. Touching that deep inner core, then dealing with and healing the issues it may expose and bring to our awareness, is but another way of moving into expanded awareness.

Meditation can bring huge physical benefits because it relaxes the body, lowers the stress level and slows down the vital signs making it possible for the body to rejuvenate in extremely helpful and healthful ways. If this is all one does, it will be beneficial because a relaxed body brings about clearer and more lucid thinking. However, the benefits of meditation can be so much greater than just the benefits that it brings to the body alone that it would be a waste to limit it. Using meditation as a tool to listen for the wisdom of Spirit, to find and see our own inner blocks and thus work with and heal the issues of the past, to find our own higher self and to allow the creative flow to emerge and once again express itself in meaningful forms, is to use meditation as a tool for psycho-spiritual growth. This benefits not only the individual but all humanity as well. We cannot change our life in even the slightest form without creating a "ripple effect" on all humanity. There are many good books on meditation and one of my all-time favorites is Lawrence LeShan's simple little book: *How To Meditate*. Here are a few simple tips and ideas to help you begin to understand some of the basics concerning meditation.

> ➢ Be consistent. Do meditate daily, even if it's only five minutes. Twenty to thirty minutes daily is an excellent goal. At times you may be seeking specific guidance, however, it's important to meditate every day, even if you don't feel the need for guidance that day, just enter into the silence. Choose a mantra such as a one syllable word (love, peace, one, Om)
> ➢ Set a regular time each day. Unless you have a time, you probably won't get "around" to it. Choose a quiet time, morning, afternoon, or evening. It's not a good idea to meditate

immediately after a meal, although meditating just before a meal is fine.

➤ Guard against interruptions. Try to choose a time when you're alone. If that's not possible, let others in the household know you're meditating and ask them to cooperate. If possible, you may want to take the phone off the hook or cover it with a pillow and meditate in another room.

➤ Sit with your spine erect. You can lie down, although be sure you're not sleepy or you'll tend to fall asleep.

➤ Don't be discouraged when your mind wanders. You will find that some meditations seem to be comprised of random thoughts. Let that be okay and just keep bringing your mind back to the focus of the meditation. Thoughts are a normal and natural part of meditation and outside disturbances are bound to occur. Dogs will bark, pans will rattle, an airplane will pass overhead, so when you realize that your mind is thinking a thought or being distracted by an outside interference that is not the focus of the meditation, just gently release that thought and move your attention back to your breathing, mantra, scripture, music or whatever you are using to focus.

➤ It is important to meditate and leave the outcome to Spirit. The purpose of meditation is not experiencing phenomena, for that may or may not be a part of it. It's important not to judge meditation by our subjective feelings. Notice the overall effect it's having on your life. Are you feeling clearer, more relaxed, centered? Judge by that. The cumulative effect of regular meditation (even when it seems mundane or full of everyday thoughts) is what aids your soul's growth.

➤ Meditation is an altered state of consciousness and changes the pattern of our brain waves. It differs from the waking, sleeping, or hypnotic state. It is unique in that it produces rest and alertness at the same time. The meditator is able to open his eyes and stop meditating at will so that any interruption or emergency can be attended to.

Creativity

Creativity can be enhanced from periods of meditation, or it can be a type of meditation by itself. In her book, *Writing Down the Bones*, author Natalie Goldberg says that a Zen master asked her why she was meditating when she was a writer. In my own experience of writing, I do understand what he was saying. When I sit down to write, I become so focused on the flow that often I barely know what I am going to say, but it's as though my fingers and heart energy take over and the words flow out onto the page. The work and effort come when I sit down to edit and perfect the structure of the writing, but the initial ideas seem to flow from that deep rich inner space. Often, I meditate first and then take pen in hand and allow the creative flow to occur. I find this most helpful if I'm experiencing writer's block, which is usually not my issue as there is so much I want to express via the written word. But even when I begin writing apart from a period of meditation, it becomes a spiritual practice and connects me with both my higher self and the greater Universal Spirit within.

How often have you found inspiration in some seemingly unlikely place? It might come while watching a movie, reading a newspaper, or participating in a discussion when suddenly one key word or phrase, totally unrelated to what is going on, bounces into your awareness with a full blown idea begging for expression. The very title for this book came about in just this manner. Weeks earlier the idea for this book had suddenly blossomed full force into my mind; it came unbidden but with such conviction than I immediately grabbed a piece of paper to outline it. It took me a full hour to outline the information that had come in a split second. It had come in a "gestalt" (a whole, complete picture) instantaneously, but it was so complete that I could have written the whole book, were it possible to type that fast, in an instant. However, even with all the information for a whole book intact, my mental processes worked overtime in trying to come up with a suitable title. One that felt "right" and conveyed not just the contents of the book but that, somehow, conveyed the "Spirit" of the work. This thinking process went on for weeks and I had a long list of potential titles but none that felt as though it were *"the one."* One evening we had a friend out for dinner, and as she was talking, she made a statement totally irrelevant to this book, but related to a Native American tradition of putting stones in a circle for a healing ritual. My mind ignored all but the word circle, and as my stomach leaped, the words: *"Coming Full Circle"* flashed into my conscious awareness. I literally *felt* the words and I knew they were exactly the ones I had been looking for and that had been eluding me until that moment of divine synchronicity; they not only expressed the content of the book but expressed what I hoped would be the *"Spirit of Truth"* within the work itself.

Long ago, the Muses, the nine daughters of Zeus and Mnemosyne, presided over the creative activities of dance, poetry, drama and music and would grant inspiration according to their own moods and whims. While we of the present day consider that to be in the realm of mythology and archetypes, we still have to acknowledge that much of our creative endeavors involve something outside of our egoic selves. While we can all learn to paint or play a musical instrument, and while instruction and practice play a huge part in our success, we also note that there seem to be artistic geniuses. These are the people with a talent or creative bent that is natural to them but totally unexplainable in terms of what we know about the human brain. There are also savants, as in the movie *Rainman,* who cannot function normally in our culture, yet, have a field of expertise that is unbelievable. I saw one on television recently that could hear any piece, however complicated, on the piano and reproduce it accurately and in its entirety. Who can explain it? In some ways mythology was right in its attempt to explain creativity.

There are ways that we can encourage our own creative flow. Like most things, we need to try. We cannot write a book if we are not willing to put words on paper. We cannot paint a picture if we don't have paint and brushes, nor play music without an instrument of some description. Saying "I can't," is equal to saying "I'm not willing to try." Creative expression is the first goal and polishing up our skill can come later. If we waited only for the genius to produce, we would miss a rich and varied source of pleasure. Don't compare yourself to the masters in whatever field you choose to express. You can take inspiration from them, you may learn from them, but don't allow your awe of them to restrict you and keep you from the expressions that are uniquely your own.

There seem to be four main stages that researchers have found in the creative process. The first stage is focusing on the goal. We explore the problem, the options and the possibilities. Once we have done that sufficiently, we enter the next stage which is the period of incubation. That time when we just let it rest and get on with the other aspects our life. In the meantime, the issue lies incubating deep within the unconscious mind and is beginning to germinate until in a flash of insight, through a dream, during meditation or when you are busy with something else and it is the farthest thing from your conscious mind, the answer emerges. And the final test comes when you find out if it will work. Not all flashes of insight are practical or workable, they may just be a step in the process to the final answer. However, you can give it some further thought, then once again detach from it and allow the process to work another time. Remember how many times Thomas Edison tried before he made a light that worked. He never denied the fact that he believed electricity existed; he merely kept refining his receptacle. So we too must refine our ability to connect with the multi-dimensional potential until just the right creative expression or answer can be received by our conscious mind.

Even though I have stated that on occasions I receive instant insights for full blown projects, those same projects may take me months or years to bring to completion as a finished product. And, as with many things, there also exists the paradox. Those times when I haven't the foggiest notion as to what I'm going to do, it's not until I sit down at the computer or with pen in hand, does anything seem to come to mind. At those times, it seems as though my intention to write is paramount and my desire to produce becomes the raw material from which my work will eventually present itself. Creativity cannot be found in a formula; it is as diverse as the Divine Mind from whence it comes.

There are many good books that can aid you in discovering your connection to the great creative flow and four I highly recommend are: *The Artist's Way*, and *Vein of Gold* by Julie Cameron, *Drawing from the Right Side of The Brain* by Betty Edwards, and *Writing the Natural Way*, by Gabriele Lusser Rio. These are all excellent sources for helping you use creativity as a way of connecting with the greater aspects of creativity through the Divine Source.

There are so many levels of consciousness and the multi-dimensional potential is mind boggling. Quantum physics has only begun to give us some idea of the vast possibilities that lie beyond our five primary senses, but it is awesome to say the least. Gary Zukov in his book, *Seat of The Soul*, unlocks some of the mystery for us and helps us understand the larger picture which I have come to call the *Cosmic and Evolutionary Perspective or the Cosmic Overview.*

Developing Our Intuitive Nature

There are so many "signals" out there just waiting to be heard. The more we develop our connection to the God Force and the more we learn to listen through our dreams and meditations, the more, it seems, that our intuitive nature develops. We all have moments of "knowing." Those times when the phone rings and we get a "flash" and know who is on the other end even before answering it, or when we feel that something is amiss with someone we love and it proves to be true; these are examples of our intuition at work. I strongly suspect that we all get far more of these flashes than we ever pay attention to, and with a little effort, we could all tune into far more than we do. Just watching the number of "co-incidences" that occur in our life is an example of extra-sensory perception at work. Carl Jung called this "synchronicity" and implied that he believed it was an integral part of higher intelligence at work in the universe. My own observations certainly lead me to agree with Jung's conclusion. The more intimately involved we become with our Higher Self or the God Force within, the more blatant and frequent these synchronistic events seem to happen. Larry Dossey's book: *"The Power of Premonitions"* is an excellent read and study of these sixth sense perceptions.

The Kahuna's, who were the priests and magic-workers of ancient Hawaii, believed that something called aka threads, which were invisible, could act as connections between people and things. Once these connections had been established, the aka threads could send out projections capable of reaching out to both carry and receive information. They believed that the more frequently these aka threads were used, the stronger they became. Of course, there is much more to it than this brief explanation implies, but perhaps it is a possible explanation as to how intuition works and how energy "lines" get established. There is no doubt in my mind, because of personal experience, that some sort of invisible transmitting energy allows us to send and receive information that is otherwise not available to us.

Once while sitting in our living room watching the TV program Jeopardy with four other friends, the category "Authors" flashed on the screen. The network then went to a station break before asking the final Jeopardy question. A picture of Nathaniel Hawthorne, remembered from a deck of playing cards from a game called "Authors" that I played as a child, flashed unbidden and only momentarily before my eyes. I blurted out: "the answer is Nathaniel Hawthorne," whereupon, my friends all howled: "sure" they loudly and mockingly retorted: "they haven't even asked the question yet," and they continued to laugh and joke about it. When the program returned to the air and the final Jeopardy question was asked, my friends Julie and Pat, who were former English majors in college, got a look of astonishment on their faces and exclaimed: "I think it *is* Nathaniel Hawthorne!" Of course that did prove to be the correct answer and everyone, including me, was astounded. Where do these flashes come from? Whether we know precisely or not, it is important to begin paying attention to them.

Because I have learned to pay close attention to these intuitive flashes, it seems that I have gained an increasing ability to receive important information through various channels. However, one of the most powerful such messages came a few years ago when I was driving home from Spokane, Washington with my friends Masil, Julie and Lucretia. It was late one dark winter evening and we were returning home via a back road. The highway had been clear for the entire 30 miles, so I was unprepared when I hit a patch of ice and the car began to slide uncontrollably. A large semi-truck was headed toward us on the two lane road. I was unable to bring the car under control although I was doing all the "right" things like steering into the slide and not braking. At one point when my car was headed into the path of the oncoming truck and it was only a matter of a few feet from us, an audible voice spoke into my left ear and said: "It's alright to put on your brakes now." My reaction time was swift and I slammed on my brakes and steered back into my lane. The car began to come to a stop and I was clearly, once again, in control of the car. I have tried often to explain "the voice." It was not my own thinking process; it directed me in opposition to my thinking about what was the right course of action in this situation. It was definitely not an inner voice. I am quite accustomed to how my inner voice sounds and works and this voice was definitely an outside one. It seemed to come directly into my left ear and from behind my left shoulder. I have only had this experience one other time and that was under a different but similar type of circumstance. I suspect that if I took time to listen more carefully when I was not in an emergency situation, I might be the recipient of more messages of all other kinds rather than just the "life and death" variety.

Deepak Chopra coined the term "synchrodestiny" which feels so appropriate to me. Here is a little exercise to help you start to experience and recognize synchronistic events in your daily life.

➢ Think of an object and notice its shape and color and any outstanding details.
➢ Remember a dream and some person or symbol in that dream. Experience it.

➤ Now in the next few days, notice if these things bring about synchronicity.

➤ Remember the more we notice synchronicity, the more it happens. Mind energy creates.

Inspirational Reading

There are so many good books that provide us with both insight and inspiration. When we read we are immediately led to the core of our own beliefs by either agreement or disagreement with what the author has written. We find as we read the penned message that there is either a deep feeling of resonance, a moment of fresh insight and possibility, or an "inner knowing" that this is not congruent with what we sense to be true.

When I find that a book I am reading speaks deeply to my soul and is confirming all that feels "right" to me, or one that is broadening my understanding of my experiences or deep inner feelings, I am immediately expanded. I always like to be reading, at least for a certain portion of my daily reading time, on this type of material as it constantly reminds me of the things I already know and hold dear but sometimes forget. It keeps me in touch and practicing what I value and encourages me to continue making serious attempts to change the behaviors that stand between me and my finest expressions of *self*. Otherwise, it is so easy to forget.

I particularly like to begin and end my day with at least a few pages of inspirational reading either before or right after my other spiritual practices. It gives a wonderful glow to my morning and helps me begin my day on a positive note. Before bedtime it gives me a chance to evaluate my day and it affords me the opportunity to go into the sleeping and dreaming cycles in a higher state of consciousness. I find that my dream life and the information and integration that comes from this level of consciousness is greatly enhanced when I am filled with thoughts of the multi-dimensional potential of the universe.

To enhance your connection with the Creative Energy of the Universe and to extend your perception of the vast possibilities contained within a more *Cosmic Overview*, you may certainly wish to take advantage of the vast number of wonderful books that have emerged over the last few decades.

Certain Types of Dreams

At this juncture it is good to point out that certain types of dreams are wonderful avenues to a larger and more cosmic view of the universe. As was discussed in the last quadrant, dreams are an excellent tool for self-understanding and integration. However, I would be remiss if it weren't also acknowledged that there are those types of dreams that go beyond our personal concerns and delve into the larger issues of humanity. There are those dreams that connect us intuitively to what may be occurring in the lives of others, often with the purpose of urging us to take some positive action. I have used the information given to me in dreams to reach out to another fellow human, and sometimes, it simply calls me to send out prayer power in a needed direction. The more we work with the dream energy and acknowledge its value, the more we will learn just how it operates in our individual consciousness. Throughout its pages the Bible contains detailed references to dreams and the role they play in Divine guidance. As a culture, we have in recent generations down played their significance and they have become, as John Sanford stated in the title of his book: *God's Forgotten Language*.

While I have had many cosmic connections in dreams throughout the years, I offer two examples as a means of illustrating what has just been said. This first dream came in the late 1960's when my husband was in seminary to become an ordained minister in the traditional mainline denomination in which I had been raised.

Dream #1

"I dream that I am taking an elevator to the top of the world. When I arrive there, I look down on the planet and all humanity. There seems to be no time nor space and I am suddenly aware that I possess all knowledge and understanding from time immemorial; there is absolutely nothing that I do not know nor understand. It became evident to me that there is not a 'random' thought, word or deed that has ever happened or that will ever happen. Despite appearances to the contrary, every event has a reason and purpose, and it is always necessary to look beyond appearances."

Upon awakening from that dream experience, I was unable to ever believe in the same way again. I eventually had to shed my traditional belief system in favor of a more expanded awareness. It would have been "easier" to have continued in the "old traditions" and stay in a more comfortable "rut." However, something about that experience would never let me return to my former state of innocence. I was reminded of the time, when as a child, I was informed by my playmate that there was no Santa Claus, and even though I wanted to continue my belief in this red suited man and for a time pretended that I did, something inside me understood the deeper truth. The cost of my spiritual paradigm shift, in some ways, was great, but ultimately, the rewards have been far greater.

The next dream happened several years ago but is an illustration of the intuitive information that we can receive in dreams.

Dream #2

"I am in a hospital on the third floor. Although he died a few years earlier, I see the husband of the teacher I had in sixth grade sitting on the edge of a bed. I start to walk over to him but he nods his head in the direction of another bed. I glance in the direction he's nodding and see his wife standing there beside an empty bed. It is obvious that she needs comforting so I walk over and put my arms around her. I start to pull away from her but feel that she still needs supporting, so I decide to put my arms around her again and give her the support she needs.

This particular woman was my "all-time favorite" elementary teacher, but it had been literally decades since we'd been in contact with one another. This dream occurred a few weeks before Christmas in 1994. Then the day before Christmas I received a letter from another friend, Margaret, informing me that her husband had recently died; I went directly to the phone and called. While talking with Margaret, she asked me if I had heard from the woman in my dream. I replied that we hadn't been in touch for decades. Then Margaret said: "Ione, she thinks so much of you and always asks about you whenever I see her. She has just suffered the loss of a very close friend and is devastated." I asked Margaret for the address of this former teacher of mine and said that I'd write to her. I wrote and we immediately reconnected in a most wonderful way. We sent many warm letters back and forth for six months and then had lunch together in June of 1995 when I went home to visit family and loved ones. We touched deeply on feelings and explored our perceptions of life and the process called death. She confided that she had tried to talk to others about her feelings and no one was willing to discuss them. We both agreed that it was hard for us to say goodbye to each other that day, and at the end of our time together, we hugged warmly and promised to keep in touch. We did keep connected and a beautiful friendship blossomed; we remained close for well over a decade until her death a few years ago. Had I not had the dream, I might not have been motivated to write, but the dream seemed to show me the direction to take. On the other hand, the dream may have just been showing me what was about to happen and its purpose was to connect me again to the love I felt for her as a child. I don't know that there is even just a "single" reason for the dream, there may be many other reasons as well, but I do know that something extraordinary happened and I take great delight in the process. Synchronicity certainly played a role.

I could relate dozens of other such dream episodes from my personal experience as well as that of others, however, this is enough to show you some of the potential that lies, often hidden away, in the dream state.

The Practice of Gratitude

To connect with our Divine nature through the practice of gratitude is an exhilarating process. Gratitude in all things seems to intensify the God Force within setting up powerful energy currents around us. Gratitude not only elevates us to our higher levels, it seems to pull toward us more and more of the very best life has to offer. It brings love, peace, joy, prosperity, health, meaningful endeavors, learning, understanding, growth and all those things that we deeply desire.

As with inspirational reading, I like to begin and end my day with expressions of gratitude. It's fun to get out of bed in the morning feeling grateful for all the wonderful things that are waiting to unfold during the day, and it is equally wonderful to end the day feeling gratitude for a comfortable bed, a warm house, all the blessings the day has held and all the glorious opportunities the hours of sleep will bring. Try gratitude as a method for touching your soul.

The Objective Observer

While there are still many other ways in which you may choose to connect with your God-Self, I will briefly explore this final method. In the *Inner Healing* quadrant we emphasized the importance of self-observation in order to understand ourselves and to aid us in the process of change; therefore, I will not be redundant. However, it is important to mention it briefly again in this quadrant because the higher we are able to ascend to a *Cosmic* viewing place, the clearer our observations will be for ourselves, for others and for an increased understanding of the evolutionary nature of the planet both historically and in the future. Observation from the *Cosmic* viewing point is not unlike that reported by people who have experienced NDE's. (Near Death Experiences) They review their lives with a Being of Light who watches with them in love and without judgment. People invariably return from these NDE's knowing that their purpose on earth is to learn and to express the same unconditional love they felt from the Light Being.

The objective observer from the Cosmic level is not tempted to berate, but lovingly leads us to discover higher ways of living life on earth. This Cosmic Observer (our indwelling spiritual nature) understands the greater purpose and meaning behind events and is a more highly evolved energy. It is a gentle, loving, and consistent teacher that is capable of moving us forward and altering our energy patterns even when the route seems circuitous. Inviting this Divine Energy to heighten our senses and increase our sensitivity, creates a solid connection and alliance between us and our own Divinity. This Cosmic Observer is also referred to as the "Watcher," the aspect that stands apart and just watches us play out our roles.

Every End Is A Beginning

As stated in the beginning, it is well to start the four quadrant process with a quick look at the *Cosmic Overview* and affirming that we believe that something greater than our finite mind might be operative in our universe and in our lives. That is the Alpha. We will also find ourselves coming back *Full Circle* to the fourth quadrant at the completion of the processes where we will tie it all together, and that becomes our Omega. It will serve us well to ask ourselves during our challenges, changes and transitions, or immediately after the crisis has passed: "How does this circumstance or crisis serve me? Where is the possible gift in this event? Has it shown me things I didn't know or understand about myself or others? Has it forced me to do things or take risks that I never dared take before? Am I ultimately better off, in spite of the pain I may have experienced or the difficulties I may have confronted during the process, than I was prior to the experience? If we can even give a half-hearted affirmative reply to some or all of these questions, then we know it has served a soul purpose. If we can't answer affirmatively at the present moment, try to stop and just trust the organic process that has transpired and hope that it will eventually reveal its hidden agenda at the appropriate time. We may often find that years later we will see patterns and meanings to the events in our life that were invisible to us earlier. Then, perhaps, we will understand the richness that we experience in the present could not have happened without the previous events having transpired when they did, no matter how random, painful and unnecessary they had seemed at the time.

We will find that when we can get high enough above the current crisis/issue, we can find a seed of meaning and wisdom contained within the event. Sometimes we will see it best in retrospect and this is especially true in the beginning. However, the more we begin to experience hidden meanings and divine synchronicity in all things, and the more faith we have, even in the heat of crisis, knowing each event is rich with hidden potential for our growth and laden with possibility for our highest good, the easier it is to accept and see the greater purpose. Even when we are seeing it through the honesty of our pain and tears. At no point was this truth more evident than when my youngest son, Allan, died. Although I still haven't understood completely the deeper meaning in his life, illness and early death, I do know beyond a shadow of a doubt that I was meant to walk through this life with him for 28 years and then to help him through his transition to what lies beyond.

The Bible says that "all things work together for good for those that love God." When we consciously love God, we are better able to see and understand the out working of Divine Purpose in all things. As we began to embrace the concept of a loving universe always working toward our highest good, and the more we are able to manifest love for the Creative Energy guiding our soul, the more we become able to see and understand the ultimate purpose in spite of the outer appearance. Before this point of recognition occurs the seed of good is still there, but as long as we deny its existence, it is impossible to understand that it might have some benefits. It is possible to block our own good through faulty perception.

Everything including crisis, is a matter of opinion. How we perceive a situation determines whether we react or respond. We can learn to see things differently. We can have a "knee-jerk" reaction or we can choose to respond with creative solutions. Taking responsibility for viewing events from different angles can give us a vast amount of personal power and freedom.

Our son, Allan, tested HIV Positive. AIDS is a terrible disease that creates havoc and pain in the lives of those it touches, and I will not deny my grief process concerning its entrance into my life. However, in reality, it is "bad" only when I believe dying is not okay. When I lose hold of the fact that physical death is part of the process of life and that each soul probably chooses, consciously or unconsciously how and when it will depart, then the thought of AIDS (or any other life threatening condition) becomes a terrifying enemy. When I am looking from the *Cosmic Overview* and am able to see that the soul cannot die, that it survives physical death, and when I realize that the soul progresses both here and in other dimensions, death loses its power over me. There are to be sure, issues to confront, grief to acknowledge and work through, and letting go of what has or might have been. Viewing life and death from this cosmic viewing space may not eliminate our grief, but it will aid in the process of release and healing.

As each of us establishes our inner identity and realizes we are each immortal, on-going souls, we lose our fear of both death and change and will view things from a whole new vantage point. Events, in and of themselves, are neutral. How we choose to see them, and how we choose to respond to them creates our reality. We can choose responses that are creative, skillful and enriching. It comes down to asking ourselves: "What choice shall I make?"

The only permanence is the immortal, our connection to the universal energy often called God or Spirit. Change and challenge are positive and keep us bumping into the unhealed aspects of ourselves while it forces us to confront those places where we need to grow and expand and move toward even greater awareness. Life is a voyage, a journey, an evolution of our souls. The real magic lies in transforming pain into creative or redemptive energy.

Creating Templates

A very recent event in my life has emerged as a clear example of how even one person can make a difference. One person who is consciously seeking to create real community and who is able to hold a clear Intention toward that goal.

As I was parking in a spot near the apartment I had recently moved into, my foot slipped off the brake hitting the accelerator instead. The car lurched forward a few feet and ran into the apartment building causing major damage to a bedroom wall in one of the ground floor units.

It all happened so quickly. I was left unharmed but stunned by the event. Fortunately, the people in the apartment I hit were unhurt as well. The damage to the building and usurping the lives of the elderly couple were my greatest concern and regret. As I sat down on a nearby bench, finding it hard to believe what had just occurred, the manager of the apartment complex came rushing to the scene. One of her first acts on arriving was a flawless response to the situation. She put her arms around me in a warm embrace and said: "I love you, and no one is hurt. Buildings can be repaired and cars replaced." It was, and still is, incredible to me that the person who was going to have the immense job of rectifying my mishap had such a loving and immediately compassionate and positive response to me.

In those moments, Sandi Pearson set forth the energy template that everyone else would follow that evening. There was not a single negative response to me. As the first responders arrived they were most kind and reassuring, echoing Sandi's exact words. "Accidents happen. No one was hurt and buildings can be repaired and cars replaced." Even the tow trucker driver and my insurance company were responding in like manner and with the very words that Sandi had set in motion. It was simply amazing. It is now very clear to me that the heartfelt emotion and the honesty of her intention, made the spoken words powerful enough to set up a positive energy field of protection around me.

In a brief time everything was cleared away and the building boarded up for the night so the elderly couple could remain in their home while it was undergoing the repairs. Sandi had orchestrated the whole situation efficiently and flawlessly.

Other tenants streaming from the nearby buildings were also kind and compassionate, and even the elderly woman whose bedroom had suffered the blow, as well as her son who arrived on the scene, were kind and comforting.

This experience exemplifies the power of intention that one person can exert when the motive is pure and comes from great loving kindness. This is one example of the way a new humanity is surely evolving.

I was curious how this loving spirit evolved, so I asked Sandi if I might explore this with her and she graciously consented.

Sandi grew up in a small rural community in Oregon where her family never locked a door when they left because as her father said: "One of the neighbors might need something while we are gone." She has always carried this childhood value of both community and caring with her, so when she agreed to manage this new complex, she consciously decided these were not "units," these were people's homes and she wanted people to feel that this was a great place to call home.

Growing up in such a small and loving environment she was free to open her heart, and despite the ups and downs in her adult life, it is very evident that her heart remains wide open as evidenced that evening when she so immediately embraced me, an almost virtual stranger, with such loving assurance. So the value that Sandi placed on the spirit of community and that of an open and loving heart had become a reality in the way she lived her life. Nothing that had happened to her was allowed to keep her from living out those values. No blocks existed in this aspect of her life. While no longer "religious" in the traditional sense, Sandi has deep spiritual roots and is open to the very spiritual experiences that always seem to be a part of her daily life. When I ask her to explain to me what these feel like, she says they are the times when she feels deeply connected to another person who needs what she can offer. She feels a warm space surround her, the phone does not ring and no one comes in the office and she can fully allow Spirit to flow through her enabling her to respond without interruption and give what is needed in that moment. Often the moment is too sacred to put into words, it is a moment she holds only in her heart.

This speaks to me of what is possible in every area and arena of our lives once we commit to conscious evolution. Once we are willing to live out what we value deep in our hearts by working to heal and remove anything that keeps us stuck in old patterns and reactive behaviors, it is then that we instantly begin to touch our soul which is the true self.

Summary

The quest to find ultimate meaning and purpose in life seems to be a universal need and a great many people embark on a spiritual journey in order to satisfy this deep longing. There are many avenues to travel and many disciplines to choose from as we seek to connect with the higher and more expanded energies of the universe. Connection to this greater Life Force is the goal of those seeking to understand the mysteries that lie beyond our finite minds.

Spiritual practices such as: dreams, yoga and the other martial arts, meditation, prayer, creativity, expressions of gratitude, intuition, recognizing synchronicities, and reading inspirational books are but a few of the numerous ways we journey in an attempt to find and solidify that Divine connection.

Action Steps

➢ Choose one of the tools listed in this chapter and commit to reading one inspirational book. Try to implement some of these teachings into your daily routine for one week.

➢ Attempt to be cognizant of the number of "co-incidences" that happen during the natural course of your daily life.

➢ Look at your dreams and observe whether or not they have any objective reality that can be verified or that end up as a "co-incidence."

➢ Choose another tool from the list in this quadrant and learn about it. Try to incorporate it into your daily life for a week. Evaluate its effectiveness at the end of that time period.

➢ Continue to read about, learn about and try the various tools listed until you have given at least four of them a fair trial.

➢ Talk with at least one person that seems to have found a spiritual path that works for them and ask them to share their process with you.

And always remember, we are made in the Divine image!

CHAPTER SIX

Putting It All Together and Coming Full Circle

Is there anything more satisfying than to come to
The end of a journey and find we are exactly
Where we intended to be?
-Ione Jenson

Now that we've looked at the four individual quadrants, let's see how we can put these four processes together in order to come full circle and have one complete process with four distinct components; for it is in using all four of these steps that we have confronted and worked with our issue on all fronts.

First, we will begin briefly with the fourth quadrant. Each person will begin by affirming their personal belief system, using the faith they have found that sustains them and brings meaning and purpose into their lives. This will be highly individualized according to your own belief, or lack of belief. Perhaps for some it might even be just a simple hope there is a solution to be found. Without at least a glimmer of hope, you would not even open a book such as this. My personal preference is to begin with the basic premise that there is a Higher Power or Ultimate Source, which may be called by many names, and it consists of an energy beyond the limits of my conscious finite mind and is greater than my individual egoic personal power. I believe that

I can call upon and use that Power, and I have faith that there is ultimate Divine Order and Justice in the universe. Whatever my present challenge I will assume, on faith, that there is some greater purpose or lesson I need to learn even if it is not visibly present or is out of the reach of my current understanding. So with the basic assumption that "all things work together for good," I am free, for now, to move on to the next quadrant.

Second, let's look at an example: Should lonliness be the challenge we are facing, let's look at the issue of loneliness in the light of the first quadrant which deals with our *VALUES*. If intimacy or meaningful connection is one of our values, let's further examine just what that would look like in a relationship and discern to what extent that is feasible. Do we visualize that value pertaining to a small inner circle of deeply personal connections, or do we visualize concentric circles comprised of relationships that are meaningful, but are based on other values such as mutual hobbies, social or political issues, or other special interests? Our first task will be to decide what kinds of relationships or activities we may find desirable. While exploring our values, we may find we want lots of people in our life, but we don't want in-depth involvement, or that we may want to participate in a variety of stimulating activities that don't call for long term commitment. There is no right or wrong, only the necessity for an honest appraisal of what we value. This is why doing some honest and thoughtful consideration, over a period of time, and writing out our basic value system is an important exercise for effective living. This does not mean that we have to set those values in cement, for as we expand our thinking and bring our life into a more healthy alignment, we may also want to expand or completely change some things on our list. However, by having thought about this quadrant and having written it down, we are beginning to be more conscious about how we operate in our daily life.

Third, we are ready to move into the second quadrant which is the ACTION step. Where do we need to set personal boundaries in relationship to our values, and how does our behavior need to be modified in order to live a life that is true to what we value? Let's give some honest thought as to how we may be contributing to our own loneliness or how we can take responsibility for helping to alleviate at least some of the loneliness in our life? We may, for example, want to commit ourselves to having someone in for dinner once a week. We may want to start a group that shares a common interest or join one that already exists, such as a group that meets for the purpose of reading and studying a book, for doing group meditation or even to play games together. Whatever activity we choose, it needs to be consistent with what we value and want from the interaction. It is certain, however, loneliness will never be alleviated if we sit and do not take an active part in pursuing some avenues that will lend themselves to the types of involvement we desire. A good book that will aid us in exploring some options is: *Women Alone: Creating a Joyous and Fulfilling Life*, by Julie Keene and Ione Jenson. (Hay House 1995) The world is ripe with opportunities, but we must take the responsibility for picking, choosing, and taking action.

The fourth step is to look at the third quadrant or the process of INNER HEALING and how it may fit into the deeper issues of loneliness. In this step we will certainly want to do some self-observation.

> - Are there particular times of the day that we feel the loneliest?
> - Do we allow ourselves to sit around without taking some positive action to develop ourselves or certain activities that would make us happy?
> - And we will assuredly need to be observant of our inner belief systems. Do we hold the belief that our happiness is dependent on someone or something outside ourselves?
> - Do we feel it is someone else's responsibility to make us happy?
> - Do we have an inner child that feels abandoned?
> - Were we lonely as a child?
> - Does that child need to feel loved by us?
> - Do we need to dialogue with our inner child and try to establish a healing connection with her/him?

> ➤ Are we watching our dreams and ascertaining the feeling tone for clues as to why we feel alone?
> ➤ Are we asking for our dreams or meditations to show us solutions that will give us meaning and purpose and ease our feelings of loneliness? This is a valuable activity.

Perhaps we will want to do a guided visualization or write out some affirmations that will aid us in extending our energy outward to manifest the deeper desires of our hearts.

We may find a journal will be helpful in keeping a record of our observations and, at the same time, become an invaluable record of our dream messages. It will also give our inner child an opportunity for expression via written dialogue. I have found that if I do enough journaling through the emotional level of an issue, then some higher energy channel naturally opens up and the writing begins leading me into solutions. Eventually, if I keep on writing, the Cosmic View begins to emerge.

With all these processes in place, we can begin to do any inner healing work that we deem necessary. While we may ultimately learn to be our own best resource for our healing work, it is also at this point that we may need to see a counselor for help in dealing with the deeper hurts or events that have occurred in the past. If this is the case, do not hesitate to find a qualified therapist to help you through the worst of your traumas.

The fifth step leads us back to where we began with the fourth quadrant and the *COSMIC OVERVIEW.* As we come back full circle to the point where we started, it may have become more obvious what the greater (Divine) purpose of this situation may have been. Let's look at some possibilities:

> ➤ Did it help us to accept the possibility that there may be an energy (Spirit) that lives at the core or soul level and that draws to us the experiences we need in order to give us an opportunity for soul growth?

➢ In moving through the first quadrant, let's ask ourselves: "did it force us to come to terms with what we value or, perhaps, did it help us recognize, for the first time, just what it is we really do value?" Knowing what we value (or what specific goal we desire to achieve) is an important step toward clarity, for how can we ever hope to achieve a goal or live a life of integrity if we have no idea what we value or what we are working toward. If the challenge we are confronting came only for the express purpose of encouraging us to clarify what we believe, for that reason alone, it has brought with it a valuable gift.

➢ Has this challenge encouraged us to change or modify our behavior in any way? Has it helped us to see how we have contributed to our own issues and how we can reclaim responsibility for our life by taking some action? Has it caused us to be more assertive, to communicate more clearly, or to relinquish our attitudes of helplessness and replace them with more self-sufficiency? Has it empowered us toward greater self-confidence? Have we, as a result of this challenge, been able to identify the places where we need to set firm boundaries, and have we been able to determine just what those boundaries must be? If the issue has forced us into doing any of the above, then we are infinitely better off for having had the opportunity of growing through our adversity.

➢ As we viewed the challenge in light of the third quadrant, did it help us to look into old patterns of behavior and ways of responding in the past? Did it help us to confront old issues or hurts that have been festering under the surface for years? Did it encourage us to dialogue, journal, re-parent our wounded inner child or otherwise find ways to release and integrate and understand? Did it help us forgive those who, through commission or omission, were involved in our wounds?

➢ And, as we continue to take our challenge into the last quadrant, does it help us to see a greater vision beyond the challenge itself? Are we willing to embrace the possibility that we drew not only the current issue but possibly all the events of our life to us in order to "grow a soul?" Are we able to see how the progress and healing that came as a result of facing our challenge and moving through this four quadrant process leads us a step closer to wholeness and spiritual maturity? Has it possibly created within us a will to know more, to understand more, and to explore the vastness of this mystery called "Life?" If you can answer even a partial yes to any of these questions, then you have found meaning and possibility in the challenge and your life is, and always will be, enhanced as a result.

Let's recapitulate. We have started with a spiritual or *COSMIC* awareness that we have a Higher Power or Creative Energy that is able to help. We have explored our *VALUES* and have begun to determine where we stand concerning this specific issue and have realized that we must put into play some *ACTION* and participate in our own solution. Perhaps we have recognized the necessity for setting the boundaries that are appropriate both on ourselves and others, and in putting our inner observer to work to explore past programming and issues that may be directly related to our current challenge, we are also employing methods (or seeking professional help) to bring SYNTHESIS and integration into our life.

Now this brings us, once again, full circle to our *COSMIC OVERVIEW.* If everything has a higher purpose, then what can be the purpose of loneliness? Perhaps it was to force us into a deeper relationship with ourselves and teach us the way to discover the positive aspects of solitude. After all, we are the only one who will never leave us; we are the only human we can always count on. Perhaps it came to help us learn to take full responsibility for our own happiness and to teach us how to create a meaningful existence for ourselves. Others may be involved, but we need to be more fluid in that regard and trust "Life" to bring us what and who we need. So often we expect one particular person or group to fill all our needs and desires, and that is not realistic. That demand is an almost certain road to disappointment and failure. Or perhaps it forced us into meeting people, going places, and participating in activities that have enriched us in ways beyond our wildest imagination. We will, in retrospect, be able to look back and find many good things that emerged from this challenge if we work through these processes and let ourselves be open to the larger perspective. Now, let's look at some actual examples of this process in operation. (Some names and locations have been changed or omitted to protect privacy.)

Revamping Her Life

There was a lawyer in a large city, busier than she wanted to be, often trying cases she didn't believe in, and married to a man that didn't really love her anymore but who felt as trapped as she did. One day, during the midst of what appeared to be insurmountable challenges, she decided that if she didn't do something about putting her life into a more constructive mode, there was no longer any reason to go on living. But at that precise moment of deepest despair, a long forgotten faith surfaced and infused her with the belief that, while at the human level her life was unmanageable and she needed help, there was a greater power that would help her find a way out of her hopelessness.

She took a few weeks to think about what it was that she wanted and what she valued enough to build a new life around. She soon discovered that simplicity and the time to get acquainted with herself were top priorities. She also wanted a physical environment that embodied fresh air, weather without extreme temperatures of either heat or cold, and where there was space and natural beauty. With this step in place, she now needed to arrange her life to accommodate her newly recognized values.

She found just the place that fit into her dream of the life she wanted to live. She then needed to downsize the rest of her lifestyle in order to leave her marriage, and she needed to seek free-lance work to replace her full time employment thus allowing her to live a slower paced and more peaceful existence. She began modifying her spending habits immediately by determining what items were basic needs, what things were optional and just which expenditures fell into the category of "luxuries." She found that she had soon cut her spending in half and was accumulating a comfortable nest egg which would help her achieve her newly determined goal. She made some sensible long term investments to replace higher risk and shakier ones, sold or gave away everything that was not basic and essential to life in her new home which consisted of two small rooms and bath, and she begin to see life as worth living again. At this point, she left her husband and job behind and moved into her chosen new environment. It was a peaceful location where she had trees and a view of the ocean. She had "critters" and birds and could see the whales and sea lions at rest and play.

With sufficient work to be both creative and to supply enough income for her very simple lifestyle, she now had time to do some inner exploration. She was amazed to discover a whole new world within herself and ardently pursued the study of dreams, learned to meditate, read a bookshelf of books that had been waiting for her to find time to read, and begin to journal avidly. She dabbled with paints and chalk drawings and reconnected with the child that lived within. She and her inner child took long walks, swam in the ocean on warm summer days, laughed and played, and began to discover joys she hadn't known since childhood. Life became both rich and full, quiet and peaceful all at the same time.

Now, several years later, she looks back at her process. She says she thinks that some Higher Wisdom, Cosmic Intelligence, or God Force Within allowed her to get herself so mired down in consumerism, in less than a happy career and in a bad relationship simply to force her into focusing on the basic values that she had buried somewhere along the way. She continues to be very happy with her simple and easy lifestyle; she has time to think, to learn, to explore and to set her own schedule and agenda. She feels that from a Cosmic viewing point, her challenge became her route to discovering herself and to encouraging her to work on learning to love herself unconditionally. In short, that she has found the meaning and purpose of her existence.

She was not consciously aware of the four steps as outlined here when she was taking them, but as her story unfolded, it was easy to see that she had employed all four quadrants in bringing her life into a healthy state. She had come full circle.

Different Priorities

Sam and Carol were having constant battles over finances. They each valued their relationship and marriage so they wanted to discern the deeper issues that may underlie their conflicts over finances. They each had a strong spiritual life and knew this challenge was for their ultimate learning and growth, but they were stuck. The problem seemed to lie in the fact that they each had a different value system regarding money. Carol was ultra conservative with money and worked hard to watch expenditures, find the best deals on the necessities in order to save money for the future; she was worried about having ample retirement funds. Sam, on the other hand, was unconcerned about saving and focused on spending money, having fun, and buying adult "toys." As often happens, they had polarized. The more Sam spent, the more worried and conservative Carol became. The less willing Carol was to spend money, the more "toys" Sam demanded. The struggle was endless. In reality, Carol and Sam were mirroring shadows for one another. As long as Sam bought enormous amounts of toys, Carol could repress her own need for pleasure, concentrate on the necessity to save, and be angry with Sam. As long as Carol worried about retirement, Sam could repress any concerns he might have about money. This allowed him to concentrate his efforts on trying to get Carol to loosen up with the funds so he could purchase an ever increasing number of toys and to be angry with her.

When people have two major values that seem to be dichotomous, even though many other values are the same, it presents a problem that can eventually affect other aspects of the relationship unless they can reach an agreement or a compromise that is workable. Dialoguing is helpful in a situation like this. Just as one would do with a sub-personality using two chairs, Sam and Carol each occupied a chair and begin to dialogue. Of course, arguments ensued first, emotions came to the surface, but from there they were able to explore options and positive actions. They finally made an agreement to take all income and, after figuring out the necessary household, health and job expenditures, split the rest down the middle. Carol could save as much as she needed to feel comfortable, and she would invest this in her own name. They agreed that when they reached retirement, if she ate steak and Sam could only afford tuna, they would both understand that this had been his choice and Carol would not need to feel guilty. Each would pay an equal share of the expenses when taking trips, dinning out, etc. They could invite and treat one another to dinner or a movie if they wished, but it was to be done in a spirit of love and giving and not because it was expected. If one of them wanted the other to participate in an event or go on a trip that the other didn't want to spend money on, then the option would be to go alone or pay the other's way. These are some of the ways they would modify the way they had been handling their money issues.

Sam spent time exploring his inner child and why he demanded so many toys in order to be happy; he seemed to have an insatiable need to spend money acquiring things that never satisfied him for long. He soon discovered it came from his lack of self-worth and that, to him, being able to afford "toys" gave him value. He needed to love and work intensively with "little Sammy."

Carol also found some of her fears and money concerns stemmed from earlier programming and had been re-stimulated by Sam's excessive spending. She also knew that reasonable investments were important. So as they hammered out the boundaries around joint expenditures, they also knew that they would each have personal funds to control, and they began to relax and be more open to one another.

After they began this division of funds, Carol took several trips and had really taken pleasure from using part of her funds. At the same time, she was also feeling more secure as she made some personal investments. Sam, on the other hand, had to take responsibility for his own funds and could no longer blame Carol for denying him what he wanted. He now had to weigh carefully what he desired and if it was worth the investment. He took flying lessons and could happily make that choice without fighting with Carol over the money spent doing it. At the same time, Carol took pleasure in Sam's enjoyment of flying because he was spending his money.

Old habits die hard. Sometimes they had to struggle when Sam wanted to make one of his "purchases" a part of their joint expenses, or when Carol would look askance at one of Sam's new "toys" that she deemed unnecessary and made a remark about it. However, they became conscious of the process and neither could fool the other; each of them had a basic understanding of the dynamics surrounding what was happening. Awareness certainly helps keep the "game playing" at a minimum because it's hard to keep a game going if the other person knows the "name of the game" and refuses to play.

While this financial arrangement is not necessarily a panacea and may not work for others, it turned out to be a viable solution for them. Sam and Carol went through all four processes:

> They faced their issue and knew it contained opportunities for growth.
> They clarified their individual values.
> They modified the way they had approached the problem. They set up boundaries around the issue and each of them agreed to honor these limits.
> Both Sam and Carol were willing to search places inside themselves and to look for reasons behind their behaviors. Each began to work on healing and integrating the blocks that were keeping them "stuck."
> Finally, each of them came to see how, in the process of confronting the issue of money in such a holistic way, they had discovered and healed certain aspects of themselves that had otherwise gone undetected. They recognized the cosmic

gift that had come as a result of releasing themselves and one another to the Divine Process and to their individual growth patterns. And, even though from time to time they had to deal with certain aspects of the issue again, the lessons come at higher and higher evolutionary levels and they now have both the understanding and the tools with which to handle it.

Doug and Clare

Another typical case scenario that I read about several years ago, is one that Doug and Clare found themselves facing. As baby boomers with a healthy two career income and three children, they were constantly frustrated that money flowed through their hands. They would save a little, and then something would come up and they would need to dig into the nest egg. Their children were approaching college age and Doug and Clare had hoped to retire early. They knew they would be able to afford either college educations for the children or retirement, but they couldn't afford both, and they felt frustrated. They seemed unable to choose between tomorrow's financial needs and today's comforts and luxuries, and they didn't seem able to commit to a plan that would allow for some of each.

The first step Clare and Doug needed to take was to see their lives from a more cosmic viewing place. They needed to realize that they could learn lessons and experience personal growth from the choices they were being forced to confront; they needed to realize that they were being given both the challenge and the opportunity to evolve in many ways that were intangible, but powerful, if they had the desire to use this experience for that purpose.

Doug and Clare's first step was to sit down and write out the values they wanted to guide their life by and that were basic to what they believed to be morally right for them. Then, they needed to record the more specific values and goals that seemed important for the next few years of their life. (Such as educating their children and beginning an additional retirement fund.) The next step was to discuss and agree on how to set some healthy boundaries around their saving and spending habits.

Clare and Doug found the places where they could, and were willing to, change their spending habits and modify their behavior concerning their financial goals. They began to take some steps, even if they were small ones, toward fulfilling their specific goals and values. Doug and Clare admitted that their predicament had been their own fault, and they took full responsibility for their dilemma. They knew they had chosen to live in a house that was far larger than they needed, and they realized they each drove cars far too expensive and luxurious and they traded them in for new models far too often.

Doug and Clare also knew they needed to commit to a more extensive and regular savings plan and to do more than talk and worry about the children's education and their own early retirement. They ultimately decided to start changing their spending habits by downsizing and buying a house which accommodated the needs of their family but that did not keep the budget stretched keeping up with huge monthly payments. They opted to get less expensive cars and agreed to drive them longer. They made a mutual decision to take fewer and less expensive vacations and to eat out less frequently each week. Both Doug and Clare conceded these were just a few of the ways, out of many possible alternatives, that they could employ to enhance their savings program.

Even though Doug and Clare's plan is a modest adjustment in many ways, it certainly is a good start toward reaching their goals. As time goes by and they begin to see results, perhaps they will decide to modify their spending and saving habits even further, but for now, they have reduced their frustrations and feel good about their ability to help finance college educations for their children and still enjoy a reasonably early retirement. However, they would never have gotten this far without some modification in their lifestyle nor without the willingness to take the responsibility for helping to reach their goals.

It would also be wise for Doug and Clare to spend some introspective time looking at the reasons that compelled them to spend so extravagantly. In doing so, it might help them to make certain they don't fall into similar traps in the future. They do feel they are very representative of the baby boomer generation and that even before embarking on their new program they were better off than most all their relatives and friends of the same age. At least they did not allow themselves to charge large amounts on their credit cards, and their house payment was their only debt.

Perhaps, as members of the baby boomer generation, their parents had been so busy making certain that their children had all the luxuries that the parents felt they had missed while growing up, that the "baby boomers" were programmed early to equate "things" with success. Also, the baby boomers were the first generation of children that was raised from the cradle with television. Television, in its first two or three decades, carried many family situation comedies that portrayed a more extravagant lifestyle than the average person had at that time, but it was one that many were trying to attain. In these programs, children got used to seeing problems presented and solved in thirty minutes, and "baby boomers" were the first generation where large numbers of people from the middle class were becoming more accustomed to instant gratification.

Clare and Doug might profit from an investigation into some basic underlying beliefs that have been responsible for undermining their goals. Clearly, some inner work could help them understand some of the compelling energies that have worked against them and sabotaged their own best interests. The more lucid and conscious we are about these energies, and make no mistake they can have a power and life of their own, the more we can work with them and keep them from controlling our lives and working against our best intentions.

And, of course, we come back *FULL CIRCLE* to our *COSMIC* viewing place where it is possible to see and understand how much Clare and Doug can enrich their lives by grappling with this challenge in a conscious way. Even though they may be spending less of their income, they might find they can create ways in which to have deeper and more meaningful experiences with their children and with one another. They will, without doubt, also find that their lives are enriched in the process. Sometimes, families who are working toward common goals share a closeness and a concern for one another not possible when they have no such shared commitments. Children who are old enough to take some responsibility for saving and contributing toward their own future, may ultimately have been given the most profound gift their parents could ever have bestowed upon them. Doug and Clare's children can profit from the discipline of saving for part of their education.

Empowering children consists not necessarily of handing them what we think they need, but rather giving our children the confidence to know that they hold the key within themselves to find ways of getting what they need and want. Thinking parents have to finance all of their children's college education without requiring them to take any responsibility for contributing to it, may be one of the biggest fallacies we promote. Those who help contribute to their college education may be far less likely to waste the opportunity. Certainly, I am not advocating that we give no help at all, however, in asking for reasonable cooperation from our children in order to help finance the cost of college, we are giving them an opportunity to be responsible.

If Doug and Clare work through the four quadrants and use the various processes, they can confront their challenge and conquer it permanently. And they just might end up with far more, both financially and intangibly, than they ever thought possible.

Adreanna

Adreanna was a young woman who was grappling with some of her issues. She was feeling stuck and didn't know what her next step should be. Adreanna was feeling frustrated because her parents were no longer able or willing to hand over the necessary sums of money she desired in order to sustain her life in the manner to which she had become accustomed, she was, in her words, "pissed."

When Adreanna was asked to answer this question: "Pretend that you are now a very old woman and your time of transition into the next dimension is at hand. Think back over your life and about what you would like people to be able to say about you - about what you valued, about what was important to you, about the kind of person you were - just what would you hope was true about you and your life on planet earth?" At the conclusion of a period of silence in which she gave some deep thought to the question, she stated that she had seen a "picture" of a young man jump up and stretch out his arms upward in a sign of power.

In exploring the question regarding her values. She felt that she would like people to say that she was understanding, loving, caring and sensitive, but in the process, neither had she become a doormat. When asked what part of herself she felt the young man in her visualization had represented, she felt he was the assertive side, her power, but that she was afraid if she let him loose that he might be capable of being hurtful to other people.

Adreanna began to dialogue with that powerful male aspect of herself, using the two chair dialogue technique. She and the young male had quite a dialogue, and she found him more than willing to act appropriately if she would just allow him to exercise some energy in her life. They agreed upon some of the ways she would modify her behavior in order to allow him expression, and she found him willing to agree to the boundaries she felt were necessary for her to remain a kind and loving woman.

She was able to confess to him that the "perks" of keeping him in a state of repression allowed her to shun responsibility. Playing out the role of "dependent child" had encouraged others, especially her parents, to take care of her financial needs. Now that her parents were tired of "caretaking," and playing the role of the "dependent child" was no longer working, she had been angry and rebelling against assuming the financial responsibility for her own well-being. He promised her that he was more than capable of helping her find ways to care for herself and that they could have a good time doing so. He also assured her that both her self-esteem and her freedom from the dictates of family expectations, in many areas of her life, would be just two of the wonderful benefits that would come from her decision to cooperate with him. They agreed that neither of them would control the other, but they would each help balance one another. By the end of the dialogue, Adreanna had not only gained some inner synthesis, but she had agreed to allow a more powerful and independent part of herself show her just how she needed to modify her behavior to allow for change. In this instance, as often happen, the inner work also provided her with insights capable of showing her just what she could do to solve her dilemma.

The inner healing techniques discussed in the third quadrant (journaling, dream work, dialogue, the inner observer, meditation affirmations, body work, etc.) can often, when used, give us important information about what we value, what healthy boundaries we need to set, and it will often give us a glimpse of the greater purpose behind our individual challenges.

In this last case of how the four quadrants work together, it is easy to see the individual steps within this one integrated example. Adreanna was unfamiliar with the process, but as she was guided through all four quadrants, thus empowering her to come *FULL CIRCLE*, she could understand just how it all worked together. Having an undergraduate degree in psychology and being on her own spiritual path, she quickly and easily grasped the concept and was thoroughly delighted to have a new tool she could begin to apply to other issues. She began feeling a bit more powerful, more committed to an on-going dialogue with her inner center of personal power, and determined to take 100% responsibility for own life. Of course, new challenges and new lessons will consistently present themselves, and even this issue may arise many times before it comes to a final resolution. However, each time it arises and she is tempted to want to return to her old habit of being cared for, but instead is courageous enough to work it through, she will become stronger, the issue will be refined, and she will gain an ever increasing sense of self-esteem and personal power.

Christina

Christina had been in "maintenance therapy" for 90 minutes a week for over a year. She definitely needed to get off "dead center."

Christina saw her challenges in the following manner: she was spinning her wheels, she suffered from depression, she didn't like her job, she wanted to go to college, and she was unhappy with her living arrangements. She was sharing a house with another single woman and her two teenagers.

As Christina began to contemplate and make a list, she found that good relationships was one of her basic *Values*, but so was independence. As she looked at her current circumstances, she could readily see that she had chosen both a roommate who was co-dependent and a job that was supervised by a deeply disturbed and dysfunctional boss.

With these fresh insights, Christina immediately determined that she had to make some changes and take *ACTION* in order to reclaim her life. She wrote out contracts with herself and stipulated the manner and the time frame in which she would extricate herself from both situations. Her contracts were: to give two weeks' notice and find two part time jobs that would allow her to take a class or two at the local college, and to find a less expensive housing arrangement and drop the roommate that she seemed to be taking care of.

Christina followed through successfully on both of her contracts. Christina looked for some of the possible reasons that she had allowed herself to be drawn into two very dysfunctional situations, and the search led her back to some early childhood abuse issues and the feeling that she didn't deserve anything better. She worked on dialoguing with and re-parenting her inner child, she used some visualization techniques and guided meditations to help her begin some healing of her past wounds, and she began affirming her self-worth.

Christina also found that journaling, working with her dreams, and learning to meditate were important pathways in reconnecting with her inner wisdom. She was also able to arrive at the conclusion that her current challenges had become her opportunity to confront and begin learning how to drop her co-dependent behaviors and create a life for herself that was positive and rewarding. As we all experience, Christina still has a few "ups and downs," but she certainly got off "dead center" and is coping with life in a far more healthy manner.

It will be helpful here to realize that this four step process is not just appropriate for confronting the big issues and challenges of life, but can become a habit that will automatically move with us through our everyday existence and all the small obstacles that come along.

Here is how the four quadrant process can be used on the small everyday kinds of challenges. Saying "no" to people used to be much more difficult for me than it is now. Out of my reluctance to refuse someone's request for my time and help, I would often over schedule myself to the point of exhaustion. When I started to realize that this behavior needed modifying, I had to determine what a realistic amount of outside activity would be for me. Then I had to determine what activities would be most productive for promoting the values I held as important, and then set some firm boundaries in order to keep and honor this new commitment of not over scheduling myself.

Simultaneous to drawing my boundaries, I began to explore the deeper origins of my reluctance to say "no." I soon discovered that my early programming had created a definition of love that said: "If you love me, you'll do as I ask." I well remember my mother uttering that phrase literally hundreds of times during my growing up years - probably because it worked so effectively. She used to read me a poem entitled: *Who Loved Mother Best* in order to prove her point. I have never thought this was a sinister or deliberately malicious act, just an unenlightened act by an under-educated woman attempting to raise her child to accept the values she, as the parent, embraced and felt was her duty to pass on by whatever means worked. The message both spoken and unspoken was, that a "loving" person is self-sacrificing in her service to others and their wants and needs, and that others always come first without regard to whether the requests are reasonable, convenient or even necessary. All this added up to either seeing myself as a loving person who never said: "no" and sacrificed herself to others, or as a selfish person who puts her own needs first. Since I also had been indoctrinated to believe "loving" was good and "selfish" was bad, it left me little choice, for I certainly wanted to be known as loving and good. For almost forty years of my life I never saw how both could be honored and that a delicate but *needed* balance could be found. Therefore, I spent my life being conflicted about whether I was really a "good" person, as in when I did everything others asked of me or, was I a "bad" person, as in when I yielded to "selfish" and did something for myself.

When this realization began to enter my conscious awareness, I found it necessary to do some *INNER CHILD* work. I mentally visualized myself as a little girl and picked her up and sat her on my lap, and I began teaching her from the truth and wisdom the adult part of me now understood. I did, in fact, re-parent my own inner child. My dialogue went something like this: "I know your mama taught you from the only truth she knew, and while in many ways she was a very good mother, her ideas were not all that enlightened. She was a product of the cultural mores of her time. Now, I am the adult who will help you; I have an expanded and more appropriate vision of what is loving and what is selfish. The truth is that we can be a loving person both to ourselves and to other people; they are not mutually exclusive ideals and here is how we're going to do it. I reaffirmed for my inner child my intentions to still be a loving and giving person and to what extent I would do this. I also reiterated for her my boundaries and the loving and polite way that we would practice saying "no" when our boundaries were being pushed or challenged by others.

My inner child and I had this conversation frequently in the beginning, and we even took an assertiveness training class to help us become more skilled in the process. As time passed, this inner dialogue became much less frequent and we both became more comfortable with saying "no." However, even to this day, we still have to talk from time to time about asserting boundaries and holding to limits that other people consistently attempt to breach. It's important to remember the fine line between boundaries that only *directly* affect us and those that *directly* affect others as well.

From *THE COSMIC OVERVIEW,* I know that in truth we are all one, and I can only love others to the degree that I love myself. I understand that what I do for myself can't help but enhance others, but if it is deliberately harmful or mean spirited toward another, then I need to change or re-evaluate my course of action. Likewise, when I am focusing a portion of my energy outside myself to support my values and my humanity, it will enhance me as well. I believe from the Divine point of view, both the inner and outer journeys are two sides of the same coin and both sides deserve to be valued and both need to find a healthy balance in our everyday activities.

A common situation that occurs in everyone's life to some degree, whether it is expressed or whether it seethes unexpressed, is dealing with the little irritations that chaff and produce some level of anger. If we find ourselves getting angry, even momentarily, at someone or something, no matter how small, try to listen to its message. Perhaps, it is telling us one of our values has been violated or that we have failed to hold fast to one of our boundaries. This is a way of walking the issue through the four steps:

> ➢ The *COSMIC* view is, simply stated: We would not have felt anger at whatever happened if we did not have something to learn from the encounter, or if we did not need the experience to reflect for us a needed lesson.

> ➢ If we have allowed a known *VALUE* or a boundry to be breached, we can play it "over" in our mind to see how we can take *ACTION* and modify our behavior so as not to allow that same violation to occur again. If it is not a value that we have previously been conscious of or does not fit into one of the existing ones on our list, then we need to give it some thought and perhaps place it on our list of values.

➢ In looking at what *ACTION* needs to be taken, perhaps we need to clarify our position with another person or set up our life in such a way as to prevent a similar incident from happening again. If it has been an inanimate object or event, and not a person, that has caused the emotion of anger to arise, we need to assess if there are precautions we need to observe on another occasion. Often, with thought, we can see just how we have "set ourselves up," and by doing things differently or being clearer about our boundaries, we can prevent it from happening again.

➢ Now, we might want to assess what, if any, *INNER HEALING* might need to take place by looking at what patterns from our childhood might have allowed us to let a value or boundary be breached. Is it our inner child's need to be liked? The fear that if we say, "no" or "stop" that we will be rejected and left alone? Is it the fear of conflict? Was it naiveté that didn't allow us to see it coming? Was it a part of our childhood drama?

➢ After doing whatever inner work there is to be done, we will *COME FULL CIRCLE* back to the *COSMIC VIEWING POINT,* and looking back in retrospect, we might want to ask for insight into the larger purpose and lesson this small incident presented to us. What are the mirror reflections that we are being shown? Are there hidden parts of ourselves that we have repressed and then projected out onto another person as judgment? How might we be doing to others the very same thing that made us angry? What can we learn from this that will help us to love ourselves and others more unconditionally? What can be done that will help us take better care of ourselves and encourage others to do likewise? As we search for answers to these questions, we will be given new insights into ourselves and a greater understanding of other people's behavior as well. We will see new ways of behaving and protecting our own best interests in an assertive but loving manner, and we will encourage and protect everyone else's right to do the same.

It will help us to better understand the evolving nature of humankind, as well as have an overview of the planetary changes that can take place as we consciously evolve into higher and higher states of awareness. And, last, we can be grateful that our personal evolvement has a place in helping to bring about a more peaceful and loving world. As we send those vibrations forth, so the world will respond in like manner.

Used in this manner, we truly do *COME FULL CIRCLE*. The four quadrant process has not only benefitted my personal life, but the lives of many others. It has also allowed us to live a healthier, saner, more peaceful existence, and in the process, has allowed us to act in a more loving manner to all those around us. Therefore, we have all ultimately benefitted and have made a contribution to the planet and all humanity. It is my belief that the *COSMIC* purpose of life is to enhance our own personal soul's evolvement while contributing to the evolving of the planetary soul. This, then, is the Alpha and Omega!

CHAPTER SEVEN

Conclusion

Be patient with your journey, the soul will
Progress at its own pace and we are
Not always aware of the timing. However, an
Inner organic process will keep nudging us forward.
-Ione Jenson

Some readers will be asking the question: "What about the life challenges that are bigger than "big?" What about those times when the event is so utterly devastating, so unthinkable, how do you use the four quadrant processes in times such as that? Perhaps these are the *very* times when we most need to have some "hold" or "grip" on a system of reality, and why practicing these processes is absolutely essential in order for us to have available resources to fall back on in those moments of deep crisis. Religion has always encouraged daily spiritual practices and exercises in faith in order to ensure that we always have the strength we need when there is absolutely nothing else to hold on to. It has been said that crisis does not make a hero or a coward, it merely reveals to us what we have bit by bit been becoming.

In September of 2000, I received a phone call from my oldest son telling me that his younger brother, Allan, age 37, was in the Oregon Health Science Hospital in Portland. He went on to say that Allan had been found collapsed and unconscious on his living room floor in a coma. At that point my own world collapsed around me. Fourteen years earlier Allan had confided to me that he tested positive for HIV. In the ensuing years it was always in the back of my mind, but he remained strong and healthy for many long years. He had been having some health issues since May, but with the finding of the protease inhibitors and the success in treating HIV with those drugs, I had relaxed and felt that it was reasonable to expect that Allan would still have more good years ahead. So, in some ways, while I had been warned, in other ways this was totally unexpected because Allan had always been a fighter and a survivor.

After three weeks of doing all that could be done for the AIDS related encephalitis, the Doctors called his father and me in for a conference and told us that Allan's T-Cell count was ONE, an unheard of number, and that he wouldn't survive such odds. They also said that should he come out of the coma, he would never have moved and would have irreparable brain damage. Fortunately he and I had talked earlier, frequently and at great length, and I knew he would never want to live under those circumstances. We also knew the first germ that appeared would further infect him and take his life. At that point, his father and I made the difficult decision to pull him off life support, to make him as comfortable as possible and to release him to move on.

We knew our values included a firm belief in the eternal and ongoing life of spirit, even though we weren't exactly certain what that looks like. We knew absolutely that he would want us to set his spirit free and not keep his body going to satisfy our needs to have his physical presence. We struggled through our own inner issues and knew we loved him enough to set him free and let him go.

In the years since, it has been clear that many areas of his life were no longer working for him and that Allan's soul had finished its business for this lifetime. Several visitations from Allan through visions and dreams confirmed the wisdom of our decision. Not more than two hours after he left his physical body, Allan appeared to me as I was lying on the couch. He was at his physical best, lean and strong, and he held out his arms to me and said: "See Mom, I'm fine, now you and Dad be okay, too." Then he gently faded from my view. He also appeared to me, as well, in a few vivid dreams during those early months after his transition, and they were always loving, reassuring encounters which have imparted the knowledge that all was well with my son.

I am certain that had I not been practicing the components of the four quadrant process in many and various forms during the years, I would never have been able to handle the death of my child with such confidence and grace. It was as my dear friend Masil explained to me years earlier about the death of her son, Danny, at age nine: "I was in the most pain I had ever suffered, and yet I was carried in the arms of the most love I had ever known."

There is nothing sacred about the order or time frame with which we work through these quadrants. In the case of a devastating loss such as the death of a loved one, a disaster, the diagnosis of a terminal illness, divorce, separation, job loss or anything where the loss and grief is so intense, so overwhelming that it leaves us paralyzed or in a state of shock, there is only one place we can be, and that is to be with our emotions, to be present with the feelings we are experiencing. I've been there in my life; I know what it feels like.

In this space, we need to cry, to be angry, to vent and emote. We might find comfort in holding ourselves or being held by someone close to us. Perhaps we need to be angry, or even left alone to experience a myriad of emotions including shock and a feeling of being immobilized. This state may last for days or weeks, and it will undoubtedly come and go periodically for months and even years. But it is to be hoped that after the initial period of shock, we will be able to begin to employ some of these processes even though we still experience deep pain.

During the deepest periods of grief, we often grasp for whatever faith we have. We seek for something that is larger, stronger than ourselves, and something we can hold on to that will help us make sense out of what appears to have no meaning. The people who seem able to do this best, are the people who have recognized and connected with their spiritual nature and have been employing spiritual practices in their daily life prior to the loss. Often, for these people, the awareness of Divine help is almost simultaneous to the event. It does not eliminate the grief process; it does not automatically remove all pain from the experience, but what it does do, is to lend strength and comfort *in* the pain and times of darkness.

My dear friend, Masil Hulse, told me this story in 1972, and I just asked her to retell me that I might share it here. In 1960, her two sons Danny (age 10) and Davey (age 7) found dynamite caps in an abandoned building located in a wheat field on the ranch land they had rented. The caps were in a can, and the boys thought they had found "gold." Being inquisitive in the ways most young lads are, they pried open the caps to claim their gold. Of course, what followed is a horror story that can be left untold here. Danny died as a result of his injuries, and while Davey's wounds eventually healed, he lost his sight as the result of the accident. It was the following story this mother told me that is truly amazing.

Masil, an RN, was called to the hospital where the youngsters had been taken by their father who found them and by a neighbor, also an RN, who had held them in her lap in the back of the farm truck as their father rushed to get help for his two sons. Masil says that she had been teaching a junior high Sunday school class for many years and always taught her students about the need to ask God for help in times of crisis. From the moment she heard of the accident, she begin praying for the strength and help to face whatever it might be that was unfolding in her life at that tragic moment.

The phenomena that followed leaves her in awe to this very day. She said it was as though the arms of God, or some gigantic energy, enfolded and lifted her off the ground and carried her through the following days, weeks and months. She nursed Davey through the long months of healing and subsequent hospitalizations as the doctors fought valiantly to save his life and then his sight. She was able to do everything a mother and a nurse should do in the care of her child. But an even more amazing part of this catastrophe was, that while she had a huge lump in her throat that would neither come up nor go down, and while she was experiencing the deepest and most profound pain she had ever known, she was simultaneously experiencing the greatest joy she had ever known. Masil puts it this way, "Heaven was so close in that time period that I would never again fear death nor doubt the existence of life after death. I was never again the same person after that experience, and while one would never expect to be the same after the loss of a child and left with a handicapped son, it was a more profound change than just the accident. It was a change that included a spiritual joy, trust and ultimately a quest and journey that has been the beauty of my life."

Masil and her husband eventually made the difficult decision to send Dave to the Oregon School for the Blind 150 miles from home, thereby in many ways and at least for a while, losing their only remaining child. While their doctor assured them that since they had a solid financial base and could just keep him home and care for him, it was not an acceptable alternative to her. She wanted him to have as normal a life as humanly possible, and the only way that could be achieved was to send him to a place where he could be empowered toward independence. Independence had always been one of her core values.

In this time of unthinkable tragedy, she faced the reality of the situation and then determined what action steps were now necessary. Over the next eleven years of Dave's school life, Masil worked devising methods that helped him find ways to do the things he wanted to do. Sometimes this meant tying him to a long rope and to a tree near the river so he could fish as he had always loved to do. Sometimes it meant fastening a bell to a rope and then to a target so Dave could pull the rope, ring the bell and know where to aim his bow and arrow when he decided he wanted to do archery. At other times, it meant she went on every field trip after he returned to the public school system, because teachers were reluctant or unsure how to handle his handicap outside the classroom.

After Dave went to the school for the blind, Masil dealt with her feelings of pain in the only way she knew how at that time. She dug holes in ground that was very rocky, planted junipers and screamed. Fifteen years after the accident when we became friends, I led her slowly, step-by-careful step, back through that time period and helped her get in touch with all the unexpressed feelings about the accident. She expressed and released long repressed emotions. In time they were spent and the emotional release was healing. It would have been better, perhaps, if she could have expressed them sooner, but it is never too late to go back and work through past traumas. However, on the other hand, she had much to do through that time of catastrophe, so it was probably essential that this quadrant was to come last, even though it might have been better had it not been quite so long in coming.

It is important to point out that healing does not mean that you will never again experience memories or pangs of pain and other emotions as you are reminded of your loss. You are healed, however, when those events no longer control you, immobilize you, or inhibit your ability to act in constructive and healthy ways. Some things are not meant to be forgotten. They remind us of our ability to survive, they assure us of our humanity, and they bring us lessons that can be used to help us through other challenges. They also teach us empathy.

If we are to regain balance, there must come a time when we confront the fact that life means change and that potential lessons lie just below grief's surface even when we haven't the vaguest notion what those lessons might be. It is at this point, in spite of the degree of the challenge, we recognize we still need to move our life forward in a positive way. This is the place where many great people have been moved to allow their suffering to have redemptive value and to find ways to use it for possible good.

A prime example of two human beings able to turn their worst nightmare into a shining example of redemptive value, with results probably even beyond their intent to do so, is the Greens. An American couple traveling with their two young children in Southern Italy several years ago, they were accosted by would-be bandits trying to force them off the highway. The father was trying to get away when the men in the other car fired a shot that killed the couple's young son, Nicholas. In an extremely unselfish and heroic act during extreme devastation, the couple donated the child's organs to the fellow countrymen of their assailants. Even the Greens had no idea where this would lead. In a country where organ donation was rare, they led the way to not only healing several people as the result of the transplantation of Nicolas' organs, but other Italians begin to follow their lead and begin to donate organs in an unprecedented way. That one example of bravery in the face of tragedy, turned a whole country's heart in a new direction and it has most likely had ramifications reverberating around the world that we may never even hear about.

There is certainly no doubt that this grief will be with them forever. There will always be an empty place inside, and they will never forget this child. Nor may they ever completely be able to release their private "what ifs."

So how were they able, in the midst of unbearable pain, to donate their beloved son's organs to residents of a country where bandits had taken his life? My guess is that the Greens had been looking at and practicing their values long before this catastrophe happened. It would seem they were so connected to those values, and perhaps to a belief in universal humanity, they were able to touch that connection immediately, look at the reality of what had just happened to them and take conscious action to affirm the beauty of life by donating their child's organs. Their faith in something more than just their individual lives, their ability to have and practice a value system, and their willingness to take action and use the situation they found themselves in for whatever good that might come from it, despite the personal pain they were suffering, is a prime example of people practiced in living an effective process oriented life. Whether this has been by design or developed more unconsciously and practiced because it has worked well for them over the years, I cannot say. But what I can say, they have shown us a healthy way to respond to bigger than life tragedies and have helped to prove that there are ways to move through personal crisis without denying our loss, but at the same time, helping heal ourselves and others as we confront and wend our way through the abyss.

For some people, getting in touch with the left brain processes of rationality will be the most difficult because they are primarily right brained, emotionally based souls. For others who are primarily left brained in orientation, the real job will be to connect to the emotional content and allow themselves to be in touch with their feeling nature and to express emotions more fully and openly. Traditionally, in our culture, this has been the dividing point between the male and female roles. Boys were not to cry, and girls were not to fight. Girls could express pain with their tears, boys with their fists. Those boundaries are no longer quite so firmly in place, thank heaven, and more women are willing to fight (even if not physically) their own battles, while more men are able to cry and otherwise express their softer natures. However, this is still certainly not the norm.

And what about the big social issues of our day and those who have been caught up in the cycle of poverty for one or more generations? *Coming Full Circle* is a four quadrant process for creating a life of integrity, and it is about taking responsibility for ourselves, our choices, and for creating a meaningful life. It's a value as old as our nation when immigrants streamed in from all over the world to seek new opportunities for creating a better life. No one came with the assumption that once they arrived on America's soil they would automatically be provided for. They came because the United States was a land of opportunity and freedom. It was a place where, with hard work and determination, people had a chance to create a new life for themselves, their family, and future generations. It is those same values the four quadrant process seeks to restore. The goal is to empower both ourselves and others to become self-responsible, not through a lack of caring and concern nor through lack of empathy, but through the desire to help strengthen individuals to tap into their own creative potential and to free themselves from unnecessary co-dependency.

Lest anyone get the notion that I am against all forms of help, let me set the record straight. I would never want us to become an inhumane "sink or swim" society, nor do I believe for one moment that there are not deserving people who need services and that it is not our responsibility to provide for them. What I do believe is, as a society we need to be providing ways in which people, from early childhood on, can learn to make choices and live a responsible and response-able life.

There are many good programs, but the best ones are those that have a lasting value by empowering people toward self-actualization, independence and inter-dependence, but do not allow for the abdication of self-responsibility. The four quadrant process does just this. It helps individuals establish a value system and acknowledge how they live or do not live up to what they say they value. It aids them in understanding some of the reasons for their actions and dysfunctions while it seeks to teach them tools for working with their inner emotional wounds. However, at the same time, it recognizes that self-esteem is not something anyone can give another, but rather something that comes from within the individual. Self-esteem is built step-by-step by meeting our challenges and finding within ourselves the strength and creativity that allows us to take control of our lives. While this process helps us understand the reasons, it is not willing to allow those reasons to become excuses for not being accountable for our choices and behavior. It has been said that "the unexamined life is not worth living."

Excessive entitlements and giveaways do not empower people. However, neither does allowing people to live in abject poverty or illness. We do need solid programs to take care of those least able to care for themselves, but we need programs that require people to learn how to take responsibility for themselves if they are able. Let's create programs that empower and require individuals to make steady progress toward self-sufficiency and responsibility. In the tradition of America, we can continue to be a land of opportunity, but while continuing to extend a helping hand to our fellow human beings, let's create programs that help without disabling its recipients.

A group of nuns in Chicago have found a way to extend a helping hand to homeless women while requiring them to learn to take responsibility for themselves. It is a very empowering program that could well serve as a model for similar programs all around the country. While they recognize that there are many reasons for homelessness, they have discovered after a decade of running a homeless facility for women and children that the most common cause is an almost complete lack of personal responsibility.

St. Martin de Porres House of Hope, run by a Roman Catholic religious order, is not the place to go if you want an easy life, but it is the place to go if you are serious about putting your life in order! They have lots of rules which must be adhered to. They have to get up at 6:30 a. m. and attend group sessions on Monday and Wednesday mornings. They must attend classes to obtain the equivalency of a high school diploma if they have not completed high school. Substance abusers must attend daily 12 step meetings, they must take classes in parenting and other life skills like learning to manage money wisely. They are required to obtain job skills and make decisions about what they will do with their lives. Even though most of the women receive public assistance, they spend their money on things other than the basic essentials, so if they stay at the House of Hope, they are required to save 80 percent of their income. This affords women, after their two year stay, to have funds to rent an apartment, make utility deposits and all the practical things that help them start an independent life. Sometimes the women complain about the strictness and even outside agencies criticize that the rules are too stringent. However, it works! Only 4 to 5 percent of their residents ever return to the shelter system, whereas, the national return rate is nearly 40 percent. Despite all the rules, the 110 beds in two facilities are always full and women are clamoring to get in.

St. Martins accepts no government funds nor any from the Catholic Church. Homeless women leave empowered and have learned to take responsibility for their own wellbeing. Why are we not using these models that work to set up more and more programs that empower?

Perhaps if battered women's shelters across the nation could provide such an extended program, they would not only cut down on domestic violence but would eventually save tax money. At the very least, it couldn't possibly cost any more than we have been paying for entitlement programs that allow people to persist in the unproductive patterns of the past.

If we could provide safe housing for a two year period of time, employ programs that call for residents to modify their behavior, deal with their inner issues and dysfunctional patterns, explore goals and learn to develop their own value system and boundaries, and at least encourage and give them opportunities to develop a belief system that will sustain them in times of difficulty, we will have established a process that allows people a good chance of managing their lives in a healthier manner. In other words, we will be, for a time, providing a structured environment that stands a good chance of teaching people some solid life skills. In the long run this is far more charitable and loving than to hand them money which often becomes the means by which they can continue their self-destructive patterns.

Like so many others, a woman who was a substance abuser for many years received SSI benefits for being disabled. This, of course, allowed her to subsist and continue her addictions. A few years ago, she was given notice she had to go on a two year program designed to make her employable by the time her benefits were being cut off. Knowing she had little choice, she accepted her counselor's offer to put her in the hospital for detox. She was placed in sheltered employment, had a job coach, and was allowed to keep the meager funds she earned enabling her to own an old car which provided transportation to her job. But even more important, she confided just how good it feels to earn her own money and her job coach was about to help her find full time employment. I doubt that this young woman would ever have taken these steps toward independence without being required to do so, and I'm sure that she'll have days when she wishes she didn't have to work, (not an uncommon lament for many) but there was a new sense of dignity, a new confidence, and a new feeling of being in control of her life.

There will always be a few people who actually prefer the nomadic homeless life, and for them it seems to be a soul choice that may be difficult for us to understand, but long before SSI and other entitlements, these people (usually males) rode the rails, panhandled, and stumbled through life. Even with programs providing shelter, many refuse and amble on their way. We need not feel guilty or responsible or the need to rescue. If programs to empower are available and individuals choose not to partake, we need to honor the choice without trying to impose our caretaking on them. Developing local or national programs that are based on this four quadrant model can be catalysts for a happier, healthier and more "response-able" society. However, before any such dream can become a reality, we need to have committed leaders who are willing to move above and beyond party lines and agree on a system of shared national values. They then need to commit to aligning our national policies and actions with those values. Perhaps this is merely going back to and actually living out the deepest intent of our forefathers in our Constitution and the Declaration of Independence. As Rumi, the ancient Persian poet says: "Beyond right doing and wrong doing, there is a field. I will meet you there.

These same principles can be used by individual families, in board rooms, by executive councils and by core groups at the center of any project, large or small. Many groups already write "Mission Statements," and as groups of all sizes begin to function in this manner and to align their actions with their mission statements, the energy will radiate to the larger whole. Thus we have the basis for an open, enlightened evolution into co-creative relationships and eventually into a co-creative society and a true democracy. The four quadrant process always provides both the individual and group, as well as the project, with a "check back" system when they come to a divergence of opinion. These growth opportunities can take place within the individual and the group simultaneously. Far too often, it is easy to become caught in the snare of defending our point of view or position instead of listening carefully and being open to learning. In Steven Covey's book: *Seven Habits of Highly Effective People*, he so aptly points out that we must first: "Listen to understand, then speak to be understood."

Using the four quadrant process helps us emerge into a New Humanity. Over the last few decades many forward thinking spiritual leaders have been speaking and encouraging us to evolve consciously. Barbara Marx Hubbard has a "Foundation for Conscious Evolution" that originates from Santa Barbara, CA. Jean Houston has been teaching workshops and seminars for many years encouraging people to become "Social Artists." Deepak Chopra in his book: *Peace Is the*

Way: holds out hope that we can evolve into a caring, loving, peaceful planet if we can acknowledge the "tangled hierarchy" and find ways to engage humans in creating loving, peaceful communities in their own lives. There are many other souls who caught the vision of possibility long ago and were a "lone cry in the wilderness" until the recent surge of greater insight and understanding of the dire condition of our planet brought awareness that something must be done. Current events are the "evolutionary drivers," so aptly named by Barbara Marx Hubbard, which ultimately force us to seek solutions. The truth is that events and challenges are just energy. It is our assessment and response to them that ultimately makes the difference.

I would conclude by repeating that it is: "the nature of Nature to transcend itself," so I believe we will naturally be forced into circumstances by "evolutionary drivers" that will force us to change both as individuals and as a humanity. It appears evident that our only choices are to continue to evolve unconsciously creating pain and devastation, or to make it easier on ourselves by consciously entering into the process of "conscious evolution.

AFTERWORD

Just a few days prior to submitting this manuscript for publication, I suddenly became very ill with a virus which turned out to be viral encephalitis.

When I entered the hospital, any awareness of my surroundings or what was happening was extremely limited as I faded in and out of consciousness. Even the ambulance ride to the hospital some thirty miles away and my admission to the emergency room did not register in my mind. The EMTS and hospital staff went into action with the necessary procedures to try to determine the cause of my illness. This state lasted for three days. None of the things they thought might be the culprit turned out to be accurate, and since viral encephalitis is such a rare happening, only the results of a spinal tap three days later finally identified the problem.

I had extensive support during those three days as well as in the days to follow. My faithful husband, I'm told, spent 12-14 hours every day at the hospital, most of it spent in prayer. My son and his family also arrived each day to make certain that I was being well cared for and to check on any decisions that had to be made. Nadine and Sharon, members of my extended family, also arrived almost daily to play soothing music, and to take care of details that might need attention. Nadine, an R.N., had arrived at our house and was taking my vitals and tending to me even before the ambulance arrived. She later told me that she'd had a vision of me whole and healthy, but felt it was extremely important that someone get in touch with the pastor of the church that Ace and I were attending. Sharon got busy and hunted until she found a phone number and made the call.

Rev. Dr. Deborah Patterson answered the call. She was in a meeting at the church, but on the completion of that meeting she headed to the hospital. When she arrived and began speaking to me, I immediately resonated and responded to her voice. I'm told prior to Deb's arrival, a yes or no was all I had spoken and no one knew if I could speak. I have little recollection of even hearing or answering a question with yes or no, but Deb's words, probably registering first in my spirit and heart and then my mind, were clear. I remember them well. I remember her quoting the scripture: "This is the day the Lord has made," and I responded with: "and we shall rejoice and be glad in it." I guess everyone was surprised and elated that I could speak. I also remember, at some point, hearing Deb saying to me: "Ione, you're a strong woman, you can do this." Because I was no longer thinking in single words but in gestalts, complete thoughts came as one flash. I knew she was right. I also knew she truly believed what she was saying, and then I knew and believed it as well. Her voice and those words played over and over in my head even though it appeared that I was not conscious.

The dimension, or level of consciousness I was in at that moment doesn't measure linear time, so it's impossible for me to know exactly the sequence of the events that transpired during those first days. What I have is a vivid memory of the incredible scenarios I experienced.

A Near Death Experience happened at some point during that time period. I well remember standing between two worlds that I knew to be this world and a world beyond. Both places were incredibly beautiful and enticing, and I wondered why anyone would hesitate or be afraid to die for there was nothing but love and beauty. I was feeling very drawn to cross that line into the world beyond, and I think it may have been here that Pastor Deb spoke those affirming words and I made the decision to stay on this side a little longer.

However, other memories surface as I remember Deb's "presence/ energy" joining me in this dimension where we were together in a "river" of the most intense, incredibly all-consuming love. A love beyond anything I'd ever known and I realized it was the universal love that pulsates through all creation. While we were in this stream, I recall saying again: "Why would anyone be afraid to die? This is such an incredibly wonderful experience." I also recall that while there, I was so aware of Pastor Deb's presence and thought: "Everyone deserves to die while being held in such love. I will never allow anyone to die without someone beside them if I can help it."

The most vivid memory is of the vastness of the love that permeated everything. I also remember going back to the crossing point between the two dimensions and saying emphatically: "This is my 80th year. The next time I come back, I'm coming across! And then I remember slowly backing away.

At some point after the NDE experience, I must have regained a short semi-conscious state. I now saw Deb, embodied and more than a "felt presence," but still surrounded by that radiant divine glow shining in her, through her, and permeating all the space around her. I looked directly into her eyes long and tenderly, and her eyes returned the look unwaveringly while still radiating with the sweetest, most intense, riveting universal love. I knew our souls and spirits were touching one another and the divinity within each of us. True Namaste. The God in me greets the God in you. Then gently, and in response to that intense love being poured out, I reached up and enfolded her cheek in my hand, and then memory of her presence fades.

The entire NDE experience was a stunningly beautiful moment in time, and even now as I search for the right words, there are none that come close to describing the beauty and power I witnessed, but my heart will never forget. The memory is as vivid today as it was the day it happened and it becomes even more precious as my understanding of what I was being shown grows. I learned that opening to that same deep love within myself and allowing it to flow freely to everyone, moves me closer to loving as God loves.

When I later told Pastor Deb that I will never see her in the same way again, she joked: "How about when I complain?" I could only smile, for since I have seen her for the truth of her being, I'll know she's just having a "human moment." And the important fact is that I have been reminded that this is also true of everyone that I meet.

In this early phase of my illness when uncertainty ran high, Deb had found a prayer that spoke deeply to her. She read it to me, and I dimly remember saying yes, yes, yes to the words as she read. She had run off a copy and placed it by my bedside. It had been removed before I was conscious enough to read it, but Deb later sent me another copy that brought me to tears as I read it. It was a prayer of deep surrender. Had I been able to consciously pray for myself at that time, it is exactly the type of prayer I would have prayed. It was as though she interceded and knew to pray it for me!

I had been walking in the metaphysical/contemplative world for over forty years, and she, at least consciously, not at all. Later, when I asked Deb how she knew to do all these things for me, she said she had followed her hunches. I can not relate it as exquisitely as she has so here are her own words:

"I know there is far more than meets the eye in our world and we are walking past much that is happening without even realizing it. Tonight on our walk, the sun was setting through the trees and John noticed a mother bird feeding her baby bird/s in their nest. We would never have seen it, but the sun was going down just so they were in profile and you could see it plainly.

I think that is what happened when you were so ill - the energy (like the light of the setting sun) was focused just the right way at just the moment I happened to be there, and the hunch was to look at the light/energy to see what was happening there and to ask you to look there, too. I had a strong sense that the next day would tell everything, and the next day when I prayed for you, God's energy was flowing stronger than I had ever perceived it - "rushing" would be a more accurate word.

I simply cannot explain it. It's beyond my comprehension and so I will look forward to learning more about your understanding of this type of experience. I am only immensely grateful for the outcome. I look forward to sitting down and continuing this conversation."

Needless to say, I do not believe Deb's presence there was a happenstance, but rather a preplanned soul event. I guess you could say that at the level of soul and spirit we were probably in "ca-hoots."

178

I relate this experience because it ties in so closely to the 4th quadrant. I have already begun to see the bigger picture and embrace all the gifts this experience brought with it. But out of the cosmic sea of infinite possibilities, all created through my thoughts, words and actions throughout eons of evolution, why was this experience drawn to me at this period of my life? What was the bigger picture behind this event? How did it relate to my past thoughts or to my current thinking, my desires, my thoughts in the here and now? Honest self-examination found at least several possibilities:

1. My consistent affirmation over the last few years has been: "I want to think as God thinks and learn to love as God loves."
2. Having recently moved to a small rural community, I had been asking for some companions either of like spiritual mind or some wanting to learn and explore a deeper spiritual understanding.
3. Since my father died when I was 16, I've always wanted to know what death was like. I used to ask, before going to sleep, to have a dream that would reveal to me just what it was like to die. I did have dreams that helped me understand, but my NDE was a culminating experience and brought me great insight.
4. I know that God has always provided everything I've ever needed and I rely on that faithfulness. I always have acknowledged my gratitude for that unfailing love, and proof of that faithfulness came in the form of my family, Pastor Deb and the people of the Smyrna UCC Church.

This experience brought to me many beautiful lessons, and they all related to the above thoughts and requests. While I am still learning, and even though there is an infinite distance to go, my thinking is closer to God's thoughts than they've ever been.

Through this experience I am also able to understand more about the immensity of God's Love, both at the cosmic level and at the human level as well. As I remember that every aspect of the NDE was permeated with love, I decided to try a challenge that Marianne Williamson tossed out. Every day look into the eyes of at least three people you randomly meet in a supermarket, on the street, or in other places and smile as you silently say: "The love in me greets the love in you." Not only does this increase my own awareness of my connection to universal love and oneness, but some priceless exchanges of energy often occur.

I've also learned never to allow fear or past programming to put a limit on love, but rather to love wholeheartedly and *purely*, knowing love always begets love. Universal Love knows no limits and we are capable of loving huge numbers of people simultaneously. The more we genuinely love, the more capable we are of loving. When love fills us to overflowing, we may keep from expressing it, but in damming up the flow, we only harm our own hearts and souls.

The Smyrna United Congregational Church, while not quite like the New Thought and Metaphysical communities that had made up my Spiritual Journey for the past 40 years, they certainly knew how to love! Beginning with Pastor Deb, they rallied around and encircled us with such love and support and, of course, prayer. This is what I wrote on my facebook page after I came home.

"I've had a lot of time to reflect and think over the past days and weeks. Ace and I have attended a wonderful little country church the past couple of years, and I have learned one important truth. Whatever the name, the denomination, the theological leanings, where there is Love, there is God by whatever name you may call Love. While I was in rehab, I was given a soft pink prayer shawl made by one of the women in the church. That shawl covered me when I was cold, comforted me on more than one occasion, and always reminded me of the "chosen" family who was circling around us with Love. Pastor Deb walked all the way to the edge with me and back, and she was with me amid the greatest LOVE I've ever known or experienced. Don't ever doubt for a moment we are, indeed, all one."

And most certainly, Divine Faithfulness never faltered. My every need was tenderly and lovingly provided for, and out of it all, a few people have emerged who are beginning to open up and explore things at a new level.

I've also learned that while I thought I had reached a point in my spiritual life and practices that was self-sustaining, and had somewhat arrogantly even said that on occasion, I had never counted on being in a state of disconnect. How grateful I am that Pastor Deb stepped in to fill that space and keep me connected, and also for all the family and friends who were sustaining me through prayer and by sending me love, light and energy.

And finally, I no longer need to ask what death is like. I rest in faith, and when the time comes for my transition across that beautiful line, I know that I will only be returning to the LOVE from whence I came.

ABOUT THE AUTHOR

Ione Jenson has worked as a teacher, a school administrator and a counselor in grades K-12. She was a co-owner and director of The Holo Center of Idaho, Inc. in Hayden Lake Idaho for 23 years where she was also a psycho-spiritual counselor. She is both a student and teacher of many alternative therapies helping people to live a more integrated life in body, mind, soul and spirit. She currently lives in Molalla, Oregon with her husband Asa and near her son Charles, his wife Pamela and her two granddaughters, Olivia and Emma. She now spends her time writing, enjoying her grandchildren and continuing her own journey of learning, growing and teaching from the heart.

RESOURCE GUIDE

There is a plethora of good resource material available. Here are just a few of those resources that I found so helpful along my own journey. These are authors who have other available titles as well, and it would be difficult to go wrong on anything they may have written.

Quadrant One: Values

Covey, Stephen, *The Seven Habits of Highly Effective People* (Free Press)
Peace Education Foundation, *Creating Caring Children* (Peace Education foundation)
Popov, Linda K. *The Family Virtues Guide* (Plume-The Penguin Group 1997)

Quadrant Two: Aligning Actions with Values, Modifying Behavior

Beattie, Melody, *Co-dependent No More* (Hazeldon Foundation)
Cline, Foster. Fey, Jim *Parenting With Love and Logic and Grandparenting With Love and Logic* (The Love and Logic Press)
Cole, Harriette, *Choosing to Live an Authentic Life* (Simon & Schuster)
Glasser, William, *Reality Therapy and Schools Without Failure* (Harper/Row)
Lerner, Harriet, *The Dance of Anger* (Harper Collins)
Meyers, David G. *The Pursuit of Happiness* (Avon Books)

Myss, Carolyn, *Why Some People Don't Heal and How They Can* (Three Rivers Press)

Quadrant Three: Synthesis and Healing

Brown, Michael, *The Presence Process* (Namaste Publishing)

Byron Katie, *Loving What Is* (Harmony Books)

Cameron, Julia *Vein of Gold,* and *The Artist's Way* (Tarcher/Putnam)

Crisp, Tony, *Do You Dream* (E.P. Dutton)

Dossey, Larry M.D. *Premonitions.* (Dutton 2009)

Edwards, Betty, *Drawing From the Right Side of The Brain* (G.P. Putman's Sons)

Faraday, Ann, *The Dream Game* and *Dream Power* (Harper-Row)

Garfield, Patricia, *Creative Dreaming* and *The Universal Dream Key* (Patricia Garfield-Cliff Street Books)

Gelb, Michael, Howell, Kelly, *Brain Power* (New World Library)

Goldberg, Natalie, *Writing Down The Bones* (Random House)

Hay, Louise, *You Can Heal Your Life* (Hay House)

Houston, Jean *The Possible Human* (J.P. Tarcher)

Jung, Carl, *Man and His Symbols* (Dell)

Keene, Julie & Jenson, Ione, *Women Alone: Creating a Joyous and Fufilling Life* and *Emerging Women: The Widening Stream* (Hay House)

Loyd, Alexander, *The Healing Codes* (Intermedia Publishing Group)

Maslow, Abraham, *Toward a Psychology of Being* (Sublime Books)

Sanford, Agnes, *The Healing Light* and *Sealed Orders* (Ballentine)

Sanford, John, *Healing and Wholeness* (Paulist Press)

Stevens, Barry, *Don't Push The River* (Real People Press-Utah)

Quadrant Four: A Cosmic Overview and Evolutionary Prespective; The Bigger Picture

Baring, Anne, *The Dream Of The Cosmos* (Archive Publishing, Dorset, England)

Chodron, Pema, *When Things Fall Apart* (Shambhala Press)

Borysenko, Joan *A Women's Book of Life* and *The Soul's Compass* (Hay House)

Brother Lawrence, *Praccticing The Presence of God* (Wilder Publications)

Chopra, Deepak, *Peace Is The Way* and *How To Know God* (Harmony Books)

Emoto, Masaru, *Messages In Water* (Beyond Words Publishing)

Frankl, Viktor *Man's Search For Meaning* and *From Psychotherapy to Logotherapy* (Beacon Press)

Hawkins, David R, *The Eye of The Eye,* and *Power vs. Force* (Hay House)

Hubbard, Barbara Marx, *Conscious Evolution* and *Birth 2012: And Beyond* (New World Library)

Keen, Sam, *Fire In The Belly* and *Hymns To An Unknown God* Bantum Books)

Kelsey, Morton, *Dreams, A Way To Listen To God* (Paulist Press)

LaShan, Lawrence, *How To Meditate* (Little Brown & Company)

Moody, Raymond M.D., *Reunions: Visionary Encounters With Departed Loved Ones,* (Villard Books)

Moss, Richard M.D. *How Shall I Live* (Celestial Arts)

Parker, Derek & Julia, *Dreaming: Remembering and Interpreting* (Prentice Hall)

Redfield, James, *Celestine Prophecy* and *The Twelfth Insight* (Grand Central Publishing)

Rio, Gabriele Lusser, *Writing The Natural Way* (Tarcher Putnam)

Sanford, John, *Dreams: God's Forgotten Language* and *God, Dreams and Revelations* (J.P. Lippincott)

Savary, Louis M., Patricia Berne, Strephon Kapan Williams, *Dreams and Spiritual Growth* (Paulist Press)

Sinetar, Marsha, *Ordinary People As Monks and Mystics* (Sinetar and Associates)

Teasdale, Wayne, *The Mystic Heart* (New World Library)

Thich Nhat Hanh, *Call Me By My True Name* (Parallex Press)

Wilbur, Ken, *One Taste, Up From Eden* and *A Brief History of Everything* (Shambhala)

Wilde, Stuart, *The Force, Life Wasn't Meant To Be A Struggle* and *The Whispering Winds of Change* (Hay House)

Zukov, Gary, *Seat Of The Soul* (Simon & Schuster)

CPSIA information can be obtained at www.ICGtesting.com
Printed in the USA
BVOW02s2157010415

394309BV00003B/10/P

9 781504 328579